870

P9-DTL-532

TWENTIETH CENTURY
INTERPRETATIONS
OF
DUBLINERS

A Collection of Critical Essays

Edited by
PETER K. GARRETT

Prentice-Hall, Inc.   A SPECTRUM BOOK   *Englewood Cliffs, N. J.*

Current printing (last number):
10 9 8 7 6 5 4 3 2 1

Prentice-Hall International, Inc. (*London*)

A Note on References

All parenthetical citations of page numbers in *Dubliners,* both in the Introduction and in the essays, refer to the new Viking Compass edition (New York, 1967), which, with its text prepared by Robert Scholes in consultation with Richard Ellmann, should now become the standard, definitive edition.

Contents

Introduction

by Peter K. Garrett

I

Dubliners was Joyce's first published work of fiction. The stories were written between 1904 and 1907, when he was between the ages of 22 and 25. This was a crucial period in Joyce's life, during which he found himself both as a man and as an artist. To do so he had to leave Dublin for a life of voluntary exile, but in his art he returned again and again to his city and his experiences there, making of them in his successive works an increasingly universal paradigm. *Dubliners*, however, is the beginning, and its emphasis rests strongly on the concrete particularity of the city and its inhabitants.

Joyce knew Dublin intimately. He was born there in 1882, and by the time he left, 22 years later, he had lived at nearly 20 different addresses in the area. His family's frequent moves were the product of a long decline from the middle-class comfort and respectability into which he had been born to a state of actual squalor by the time he had reached adolescence. This experience helped to alienate the young Joyce from his family, whose authority he gradually rejected as he later rejected that of his religion and his country. Joyce received all his formal education from the Jesuits, at Clongowes Wood, Belvedere, and University Colleges. From them he derived a rigorous intellectual discipline and a sense of his artistic vocation as a kind of secular priesthood in place of the religious vocation he seems to have considered for a time. As a young, would-be artist in his years at University College, he rejected the claims of Irish literary nationalism, asserting the superiority of current Continental modes, particularly in the example of Ibsen, whom he admired for his "lofty impersonal power." [1] By the time he received his degree in 1902, Joyce had arrived at the position

---

[1] Joyce described this quality as "your highest excellence" in the letter he wrote to Ibsen in 1901. All quotations from *Letters of James Joyce* (New York: The Viking Press, Inc.; London: Faber & Faber Ltd.) reprinted by permission of the publishers. Copyright © 1957, 1966 by the Estate of James Joyce. This reference appears in Volume I, edited by Stuart Gilbert, pp. 51–52.

that he later expressed in the defiant words of Stephen Dedalus in *A Portrait of the Artist as a Young Man*:

> I will not serve that in which I no longer believe whether it call itself my home, my fatherland or my church: and I will try to express myself in some mode of life or art as freely as I can, using for my defense the the only arms I allow myself to use—silence, exile, and cunning.[2]

Exile seemed a particular necessity, and in 1902 and 1903 Joyce made two abortive attempts at living alone in Paris. In 1904 he left Dublin again, but not alone. With him went Nora Barnacle, a woman who was unlike him in almost every respect but whose solid simplicity was an indispensable counterweight to his unstable complexity. She loyally remained with him for the rest of his life, becoming the mother of his two children, his wife, and, in *Ulysses* and *Finnegans Wake,* the basis for his image of essential femininity. Before his departure Joyce had written three of the *Dubliners* stories ("The Sisters," "Eveline," and "After the Race"), which were published in *The Irish Homestead*. He wrote the rest while struggling to support himself, Nora, and the son born in 1905 by teaching English in Pola and Trieste. A preliminary version of the collection, containing 12 stories, was accepted by the London publisher Grant Richards in February, 1906. "Two Gallants" and "A Little Cloud" were soon added; "The Dead" was written in the following year. *Dubliners* was not actually published, however, until June, 1914. The long delay was caused first by the objections of the printer and publisher to passages which were mildly profane or suggestive, such as the occasional use of the word "bloody" or references to a woman who "cast bold glances . . . and changed the position of her legs often." Joyce insisted on the artistic necessity of every detail. He did offer to make some changes but bitterly lamented the resulting "mutilation" of his work. Even these concessions failed to satisfy Richards, who finally rejected the book altogether. It was then offered to and refused by several other publishers until 1909, when the Dublin publishers, Maunsel and Company, accepted and printed it, only to reverse their decision and destroy all the copies. This time the objections were to Joyce's use of real names and places, which prompted fear of libel actions. At last, after more publishers' rejections, *Dubliners* was accepted again by Grant Richards, who finally published it after a delay of eight years.

In the meantime Joyce had produced the long, autobiographical

---

[2] All quotations from James Joyce, *A Portrait of the Artist as a Young Man* (New York: The Viking Press, Inc.; London: Jonathan Cape Limited, 1964) reprinted by permission of the publishers, The Society of Authors as the literary representative of the Estate of the late James Joyce, and the Executors of the James Joyce Estate. This reference appears on pages 246–47.

narrative called *Stephen Hero* and then refined it into his first novel, *A Portrait of the Artist as a Young Man,* which was published serially in 1914–15 and in 1916 as a book. From this time onward, Joyce received increasing recognition as a major artist and, before long, the support of generous patrons. He moved from Trieste to Zurich during World War I and to Paris afterwards, working from 1914 to 1921 on his complex, epical novel, *Ulysses,* which was published in 1922. The next 17 years were devoted to his last and most ambitious work, the encyclopedic, multi-lingual *Finnegans Wake* (1939). After the fall of France in 1940, Joyce and his family returned to Zurich, where he died in 1941.

II

In the course of his long struggle with reluctant publishers, Joyce wrote many letters defending the artistic integrity of *Dubliners.* Of these, the following gives the fullest description of his method and purpose:

> My intention was to write a chapter of the moral history of my country and I chose Dublin for the scene because that city seemed to me the centre of paralysis. I have tried to present it to the indifferent public under four of its aspects: childhood, adolescence, maturity and public life. The stories are arranged in this order. I have written it for the most part in a style of scrupulous meanness and with the conviction that he is a very bold man who dares to alter in the presentment, still more to deform, whatever he has seen and heard. I cannot do more than this. I cannot alter what I have written.[3]

We should bear in mind the controversial context of this statement. Joyce emphasizes his serious moral purpose in response to complaints about the stories' alleged indecencies. He affirms an aesthetic of inflexible reportorial naturalism, avoiding the question of what is *selected* for "presentment," in response to demands for revisions. But in spite of these distorting circumstances, Joyce's statement provides a remarkably accurate indication of the theme and structure of *Dubliners.*

The theme of paralysis is introduced at the outset with the actual paralysis of the old priest in "The Sisters." To the boy who tells the story, the word itself carries both a threat and a kind of fascination: "it sounded to me like the name of some maleficent and sinful being. It filled me with fear, and yet I longed to be nearer to it and to look

---

[3] *Letters,* II, ed. Richard Ellmann (New York: The Viking Press, Inc.; London: Faber & Faber Ltd., 1966), p. 134.

upon its deadly work" (9).[4] The successive stories develop variations on this central theme, displaying the "deadly work" of spiritual paralysis in the individual and in the community. It is clearly present in the motionless figure of Eveline, "passive, like a helpless animal" (41), unable to accept the chance of new life she is offered. But it is equally present in the mechanical action of "Counterparts," where characters are joined only in the struggle for domination and the transfer of humiliation. Paralysis is revealed in the emptiness which lies behind the façade of dead forms, the clichés which substitute for thought, whether the romantic clichés of "Araby" or the religious clichés of "Grace." It appears in the sterile lives of characters as different as the humble Maria of "Clay" and the aloof, superior Mr. Duffy of "A Painful Case."

The most frequent form of paralysis is captivity, both imposed by the deadening environment and produced by the characters' own moral weaknesses. Joyce, the artist who achieved self-realization by leaving Ireland, repeatedly writes of characters who can only dream of escape. For the boys of "An Encounter" and "Araby" the dream dwells on the Wild West or the exotically named bazaar, but the quests for "adventures" end in frustration or disappointment. Eveline cannot bring herself to escape to Argentina; in "The Boarding House" Bob Doran longs "to ascend through the roof and fly away to another country" (67–68) but is instead trapped into marriage. Already married, Little Chandler in "A Little Cloud" dreams of becoming a poet and escaping to London, "to live bravely like Gallaher" (83), and in "The Dead" Gabriel Conroy thinks of going to the Continent to escape Irish provincialism. Repeatedly the impulse toward escape is frustrated; paralysis is reasserted. The characteristic motion of Joyce's Dubliners is not linear flight away from their stifling city but a circular motion, like the obsessive speech of the pervert in "An Encounter," "slowly circling round and round in the same orbit" (26). The same circle of captivity is described by Lenehan's wanderings in "Two Gallants" and is acted out by Gabriel Conroy as he tells the story of the old horse that went round and round the monument (208). It is the pattern of lives caught in the deadly, paralyzing round of obsession or habit.

The structure of *Dubliners* is determined by the "four aspects" under which Joyce arranged his stories: childhood ("The Sisters," "An Encounter," and "Araby"), adolescence ("Eveline," "After the Race," "Two Gallants," and "The Boarding House"), maturity ("A Little

[4] All quotations from James Joyce, *Dubliners* (New York: The Viking Press, Inc.; London: Jonathan Cape Limited, 1967) reprinted by permission of the publishers, The Society of Authors as the literary representative of the Estate of the late James Joyce, and the Executors of the James Joyce Estate. Originally published by B. W. Huebsch, Inc., in 1916. All rights reserved.

Cloud," "Counterparts," "Clay," and "A Painful Case"), and public life ("Ivy Day in the Committee Room," "A Mother," and "Grace"). Joyce's arrangement clearly creates a progression, an expanding perspective, moving from childhood to maturity and from private to public life. The moral paralysis of Dublin is first seen from the child's limited, naïve point of view, to which it appears (in the figures of the paralyzed priest of "The Sisters" and the pervert of "An Encounter") as something mysterious because not yet experienced or understood. When the mystery is finally penetrated at the end of "Araby," it is exposed as mere shabby vanity. The stories of the next group present adolescence as the threshold of paralysis. They focus on characters in the moment of becoming trapped (Eveline and Bob Doran) or in the dawning recognition of futility (Jimmy Doyle and Lenehan). The third group presents characters who are already trapped in the sterile circle of their lives, whether they come to realize it (Little Chandler and Mr. Duffy) or not (Farrington and Maria). The last group displays the paralysis of the entire community. Joyce's irony becomes less grim, more comic as he presents the Dublin versions of politics ("Ivy Day in the Committee Room"), "culture" ("A Mother"), and religion ("Grace"). "The Dead" was written after the other stories and stands somewhat apart from them. Structurally, it functions as an epilogue, summarizing and perhaps qualifying the principal themes of the entire collection.

III

Joyce's central theme of paralysis and the structural progression with which he developed it clearly make *Dubliners* more unified than the typical collection of short stories. Many recent critics have argued (or assumed), however, that both the book as a whole and the individual stories are unified and convey their meaning in ways far more intricate and subtle than those I have described. The first readers of *Dubliners* took the stories as naturalistic sketches, thin slices of life whose meaning lay on the surface. This is the view implicit in the publishers' concern with Joyce's transcription of coarse speech and real names, but it is also implicit in the response of more sophisticated and appreciative contemporaries. Ezra Pound, in an early review, praised *Dubliners* for the "freedom from sloppiness" of its "clear hard prose." He considered Joyce "a realist" in the tradition of Flaubert, one who "gives the thing as it is." Pound recognized that Joyce was concerned with more than the concrete particulars of his city: "He gives us things as they are, not only for Dublin, but for every city. . . . That is to say, the author is quite capable of dealing with things about him, and dealing directly, yet these details do not engross him, he is capable of getting at the universal element beneath them." [5] But for Pound this "universal element" simply consisted in the representative nature of the subjects selected. Only in the light of Joyce's later development did the mode of *Dubliners* begin to seem more than naturalistic.

Of all Joyce's later works, *Ulysses* has exerted by far the greatest influence on critical views of *Dubliners*. It too is filled with details of Dublin's places and characters, several of whom appear in both works. Yet in spite of such similarities and in spite of the importance of naturalism in *Ulysses,* its radical stylistic experiments indicated a far more complex method. Stuart Gilbert's influential study, *James Joyce's "Ulysses"* (1930), written with Joyce's guidance, described that method as one of unprecedentedly complicated symbolism. Not only its parallels with the *Odyssey,* intimated by the title, but an elaborate scheme of symbols, techniques, colors, arts, and organs were presented as underlying the naturalistic surface and determining its contours. According to Gilbert,

> The meaning of *Ulysses* . . . is not to be sought in any analysis of the acts of the protagonists or the mental make-up of the characters; it is, rather, implicit in the technique of the various episodes, in nuances of language, in the thousand and one correspondences and allusions with which the book is studded.[6]

To many readers this view, if accepted, would clearly indicate profound differences between the mode of *Ulysses* and that of *Dubliners*; to some, however, it has suggested previously unsuspected similarities.

It is normal for students of an author's development to look in his early works for anticipations of his later methods and themes. To several students of Joyce the anticipation has seemed virtually complete; *Dubliners* has been subjected to the exegetical methods developed for *Ulysses*. The first attempt at such a reading was made by Richard Levin and Charles Shattuck in "First Flight to Ithaca" (1944).[7] They argued at length that *Dubliners,* like *Ulysses,* is based on parallels with the *Odyssey*. Although few students have fully accepted this thesis, it has served as a stimulus or point of departure for several studies which

[5] "*Dubliners* and Mr James Joyce," in *Literary Essays of Ezra Pound,* ed. T. S. Eliot (London, 1954), pp. 399–401. First published in *The Egoist,* I (July 15, 1914). Copyright © 1918 by Ezra Pound. Reprinted by permission of New Directions Publishing Corporation and Faber & Faber Ltd.

[6] *James Joyce's "Ulysses"* (New York: Vintage Books; London: Faber & Faber Ltd., 1960), pp. 8–9. Reprinted by permission of Alfred A. Knopf, Inc., and Faber & Faber Ltd.

[7] First published in *Accent,* the article is reprinted in *James Joyce: Two Decades of Criticism,* ed. Seon Givens (New York: Vanguard Press, Inc., 1948), pp. 47–94.

have also attempted to interpret *Dubliners* in terms of some "secret technique" or hidden symbolism. Among the essays in this volume, this approach is represented most clearly by Brewster Ghiselin's extensive study of symbolic patterns in *Dubliners* as a whole and by Ben L. Collins' study of "Araby." Joyce's critics are far from unanimous acceptance of such symbolic interpretations, however, as may be seen in the scepticism of S. L. Goldberg. There is as yet no critical agreement on how to read *Dubliners*.

If we turn from the disparate responses of Joyce's critics to look for evidence of his own intentions, we shall find grounds for both naturalistic and symbolic interpretations. On the one hand, there is the Joyce who displays an obsessive concern with literal accuracy, writing from Trieste to his brother in Dublin in order to verify incidental details in his stories:

> Please send me the information I ask you for as follows:
> *The Sisters:* Can a priest be buried in a habit?
> *Ivy Day in the Committee Room*—Are Aungier St and Wicklow in the Royal Exchange Ward? Can a municipal election take place in October?
> *A Painful Case*—Are the police at Sydney Parade of the *D* division? Would the city ambulance be called out to Sydney Parade for an accident? Would an accident at Sydney Parade be treated at Vincent's Hospital?
> *After the Race*—Are the police supplied with provisions by government or by private contracts?
> Kindly answer these questions as quickly as possible.[8]

Similarly, he called his publisher's attention to his naturalistic effects, "the special odour of corruption which, I hope, floats over my stories," or again, "the odour of ashpits and old weeds and offal [which] hangs round my stories." He even anticipated critical reception as "the 'Irish Zola.' "[9]

On the other hand, there is the Joyce who deliberately inserted metaphors and symbols into his stories for thematic amplification. We can observe this procedure in Joyce's revisions of "The Sisters." [10] The first version of the story does not specify the nature of the priest's illness. The emphasis on "the word *paralysis*" in the opening paragraph of the revised story clearly introduces the central theme of the entire volume and presents the diseased priest as a symbol of a larger condition. Joyce

---

[8] *Letters*, II, 109.
[9] *Letters*, II, 123; I, 64; II, 137.
[10] These revisions are considered in detail by Marvin Magalaner, in *Time of Apprenticeship: The Fiction of Young James Joyce* (New York: Abelard-Schuman Limited, 1959), pp. 73–86. Magalaner also reprints the 1904 version of "The Sisters" as an appendix.

also added passages which associate the young boy with the role of priest. One is the dream in which the old priest comes to the boy to confess and be absolved. This would seem to prepare for the symbolism of a later addition, the scene in which the sisters offer sherry and cream crackers to the boy and his aunt. If, as seems likely, an analogy with the wine and wafer of Communion is intended here, then the boy's refusal of the crackers and acceptance of the wine would imply his priest-like status since only the wafer is offered to the laity, while the wine is reserved for the priest.

The symbolic intention of these additions seems fairly clear, but how are they to be interpreted? Does the association of the boy with priesthood imply a future of failure and paralysis like those of Father Flynn? Or does it rather foretell his destiny as "priest of eternal imagination," as Stephen Dedalus conceives the artist's role in the *Portrait?* [11] The coherence of this symbolism and its importance in the story remain open to question. The fact that Joyce has deliberately put the symbols in does not obligate the reader to extract them unless their artistic relevance can be shown. Beyond the question of individual symbols there lies that of systematic symbolism. We may grant the sacramental significance of the sherry and cream crackers in a story which is so much concerned with priesthood, but is the same significance to be found in every mention of food and drink? Several critics have made such an assumption, but its validity is by no means clear.

Elements of the stories require both sorts of reading. Several objects and images clearly demand symbolic interpretation, such as the harp that appears briefly in "Two Gallants," which, "heedless that her coverings had fallen about her knees, seemed weary alike of the eyes of strangers and of her master's hands" (54). The dishonored harp is clearly an analogue for the servant girl, who appears only a few lines later. Since the harp is also a traditional emblem of Ireland, the analogy is extended to the present degraded state of the nation. ("Yet still in her darkness doth Erin lie sleeping," runs one line of "Silent, O Moyle," the Thomas Moore ballad which the harpist is playing.) Like the "small gold coin" which is ostentatiously thrust before the reader's eyes at the end of the story, the harp is insistently symbolic. Other objects which are presented no less insistently seem, nevertheless, to be irreducibly actual, random fragments of reality, like the "plate of peas" which Lenehan consumes in the same story (57), or the "late

---

[11] *A Portrait of the Artist,* p. 221. External evidence would seem to make the latter interpretation more likely. The boy of the first three stories seems to be an early version of the artist hero, a preliminary study for the quasi-autobiographical figure of Stephen Dedalus. Joyce called these "stories of my childhood" (*Letters,* II, 111), and the boy displays those tendencies toward alienation and romanticism which are developed further in the childhood sections of the *Portrait.* Nevertheless, such significance is hardly realized within the story itself.

tenant's rusty bicycle pump" mentioned at the beginning of "Araby" (29).[12] Even when the symbolic relevance of a detail is fairly clear, it does not necessarily follow that its symbolism is its most important aspect. Consider the case of Mr. Browne in "The Dead." There is strong external evidence of Joyce's association of the color brown with the condition of paralysis.[13] He has the character himself call attention to the color his name denotes: when Aunt Julia says that the pudding is "not quite brown enough," he replies, "—Well, I hope . . . that I'm brown enough for you because, you know, I'm all brown" (200). Thus, we may find ominous thematic overtones in the interchange that occurs when the guests are departing:

—Browne is out there, Aunt Kate, said Mary Jane.
—Browne is everywhere, said Aunt Kate, lowering her voice. (206)

It may seem to convey the same symbolic implication present in the motif "snow was general all over Ireland" (211, 223): paralysis is pervasive. Yet it is eminently arguable that Mr. Browne's realistic aspect remains more significant than these symbolic suggestions, that in his jovial, crude vitality he displays a human substantiality which resists being reduced to a simple, symbolic image. Interpretations of *Dubliners* will be affected considerably by the reader's view of the relationship between such symbolic and naturalistic elements, his sense of which determines meaning.

Concern with this very problem emerges in "The Dead," which, as epilogue, recapitulates not only the themes but the methods of *Dubliners.* The issue comes into focus in a brief scene which takes place as various guests are leaving the party.

Gabriel had not gone to the door with the others. He was in a dark part of the hall gazing up the staircase. A woman was standing near the top of the first flight, in the shadow also. He could not see her face but he could see the terracotta and salmonpink panels of her skirt which the shadow made appear black and white. It was his wife. She was leaning

[12] Like nearly every other detail of *Dubliners,* these have also been given symbolic interpretations, the bicycle pump by Ben L. Collins in the essay reprinted below, and Lenehan's peas by Robert S. Ryf, in *A New Approach to Joyce: The "Portrait of the Artist" as Guidebook* (Berkeley and Los Angeles: University of California Press, 1964), p. 67. The fact that such interpretations have been made does not prove their appropriateness, however.
[13] E.g., the reference to "those brown brick houses which seem the very incarnation of Irish paralysis," in *Stephen Hero,* p. 188. Cf. the houses at the beginning of "Araby" which "gazed at one another with brown imperturbable faces" (29). All quotations from James Joyce, *Stephen Hero* (London: Jonathan Cape Limited, 1944) reprinted by permission of the publisher, the Executors of the James Joyce Estate, and The Society of Authors as the literary representative of the Estate of the late James Joyce.

on the banisters, listening to something. Gabriel was surprised at her stillness and strained his ear to listen also. But he could hear little save the noise of laughter and dispute on the front steps, a few chords struck on the piano and a few notes of a man's voice singing.

He stood still in the gloom of the hall, trying to catch the air that the voice was singing and gazing up at his wife. There was grace and mystery in her attitude as if she were a symbol of something. He asked himself what is a woman standing on the stairs in the shadow, listening to distant music, a symbol of. If he were a painter he would paint her in that attitude. Her blue felt hat would show off the bronze of her hair against the darkness and the dark panels of her skirt would show off the light ones. *Distant Music* he would call the picture if he were a painter. (209–10)

By the end of the story this distanced, impersonal mode of contemplation has been destroyed. Gabriel is forced to realize that his wife is not an aesthetic object, "a symbol of something," but an actual person whose individuality and otherness must be respected. The retrospective irony of the scene would thus appear to be directed entirely against the attempt to convert reality into symbol. It might even be taken as a kind of warning to critics who attempt to impose symbolic interpretations on Joyce's stories. Yet the situation is more complex, for the scene is indeed symbolic, though in a different sense from that which Gabriel intends. It gathers in a single dramatic image the crucial factors in the deficient relationship of the Conroys, juxtaposing Gabriel's self-regarding, mild aestheticism with Gretta's abstracted thoughts of another, her memory of a greater love than he can offer. The distant music to which she is listening reminds her of Michael Furey, who died for love of her, and it is the revelation of this part of her past that exposes the shallowness of Gabriel's attitude, forcing him to recognize his wife as a person.

This passage points forward to the Joyce of the *Portrait* and *Ulysses,* the artist who uses symbolic techniques to explore the relation between symbolism and naturalism, between art and reality. But it also points back toward the earlier stories of *Dubliners,* indicating a fictional mode which moves between the extreme limits of literal naturalism and a completely determined or systematic symbolism. It is in the latter mode that the object becomes "a symbol of something," equated with a fixed meaning as in allegory. The stories of *Dubliners* do at times make such allegorical equations, such as that of the harp (in "Two Gallants") with the girl and with Ireland. More often, however, they develop situations which are symbolic in the manner of the "Distant Music" scene from "The Dead," dramatic complexes which suggest but do not insist on a larger significance.

IV

The fictional method by which Joyce mediates between naturalism and symbolism in *Dubliners* may be seen as the consequence of his notion of the epiphany. Like Joyce's conception of the artist as priest, the term arises from the aesthetic displacement of religious vocabulary. Originally referring to the revelation of the infant Jesus to the Magi, it becomes a kind of artistic revelation. For Joyce, the epiphany was an experience before it became an artistic strategy, and it is as such that he defined it in *Stephen Hero*:

> By an epiphany he [Stephen Daedalus] meant a sudden spiritual mani-
> festation, whether in the vulgarity of speech or of gesture or in a memor-
> able phase of the mind itself. He believed it was for the man of letters
> to record these epiphanies with extreme care, seeing that they themselves
> are the most delicate and evanescent of moments.[14]

Joyce himself recorded such moments, fragments of dialogue or personal experience which struck him as "spiritual manifestations." [15] The content manifested in such moments was usually some form of spiritual deficiency; the epiphany thus acquired strong connotations of ironic exposure. At first the exposure involved only the individuals observed. According to his brother, Joyce thought of his epiphanies as psychological slips, "little errors and gestures—mere straws in the wind —by which people betrayed the very things they were most careful to conceal." [16] But as Joyce began to use such moments as material for his fiction, he found them capable of revealing much more. At an early point in the composition of *Dubliners* he wrote to a friend, "I am writing a series of epicleti—ten—for a paper. I have written one. I call the series *Dubliners* to betray the soul of that hemiplegia or paralysis which many consider a city." [17] From the outset, Joyce conceived of his method as the ironic, epiphanic exposure of his central theme.

[14] *Stephen Hero*, p. 188.
[15] All the surviving records of such epiphanies are reprinted in *The Workshop of Daedalus*, ed. Robert Scholes and Richard M. Kain (Evanston: Northwestern University Press, 1965), pp. 11–51.
[16] Stanislaus Joyce, *My Brother's Keeper* (New York: McGraw-Hill Book Company, 1958), p. 124.
[17] *Letters*, I, 55. *Epiclesis* (for which the correct plural form is *epicleses*) is the ritual invocation asking the Holy Ghost to transform the host into the body and blood of Christ. Joyce conceives of himself as artist-priest, "converting the bread of everyday life into something that has a permanent artistic life of its own." See *My Brother's Keeper*, pp. 103–4, and Richard Ellmann, *James Joyce* (New York: Oxford University Press, 1959), p. 169.

To understand the techniques by which he achieved that exposure, we should return to the passage in *Stephen Hero* where the idea of the epiphany first appears. It is prompted by a "trivial incident": Stephen observes a young couple talking before "one of those brown brick houses which seem the very incarnation of Irish paralysis" and overhears the following "fragment of colloquy":

> The Young Lady—(drawling discreetly) . . . O, yes . . . I was . . . at the . . . cha . . . pel . . .
> The Young Gentleman—(inaudibly) . . . I . . . (again inaudibly) . . . I . . .
> The Young Lady—(softly) . . . O . . . but you're . . . ve . . . ry . . . wick . . . ed . . .[18]

To Stephen this brief dialogue, in its triviality and affectation, also appears as an "incarnation," a concrete embodiment of Irish moral paralysis. The epiphanies which Joyce collected frequently record such moments. In isolation they reveal very little, but when placed in the context of a fictional structure, these fragments of a drab reality can become charged with significance. According to Stephen, "the artist who could disentangle the subtle soul of the image from its mesh of defining circumstances most exactly and re-embody it in artistic circumstances chosen as most exact for it in its new office, he was the supreme artist."[19] This is what Joyce did in selecting his epiphanies and then incorporating them in a fictional context.

A minor example may be seen in a fragment of dialogue, quite similar to the passage in *Stephen Hero,* which occurs near the end of "Araby." Having finally arrived at the bazaar, the boy approaches one of the stalls, where "a young lady was talking with two young gentlemen" and overhears their conversation:

> —O, I never said such a thing!
> —O, but you did!
> —O, but I didn't!
> —Didn't she say that?
> —Yes. I heard her.
> —O, there's a . . . fib! (35)

This moment contributes to the exposure of the empty banality which lies behind the exotic façade of the name "Araby." It replaces the boy's fantasies of love in terms of chivalric romance with the trivial actuality of ordinary flirtation, deflating his romantic dreams. In its fictional context this fragment of reality becomes a minor revelation.[20]

[18] *Stephen Hero*, p. 188.
[19] *Stephen Hero*, p. 65.
[20] The passage is not in fact one of the extant epiphanies, but it is easily recognizable as the sort of observation the young Joyce recorded. None of the

Joyce also uses such brief scenes to create more portentous revelations. An example is the ending of "The Sisters," which reveals the crucial event in the dead priest's past—his breaking of the chalice and its effect on him—and also, equally important, the uncomprehending attitude of those around him:

> And what do you think but there he was, sitting up by himself in the dark in his confession-box, wide-awake and laughing-like softly to himself?
>
> She stopped suddenly as if to listen. I too listened; but there was no sound in the house: and I knew that the old priest was lying still in his coffin as we had seen him, solemn and truculent in death, an idle chalice on his breast.
>
> Eliza resumed:
>
> —Wide-awake and laughing-like to himself. . . . So then, of course, when they saw that, that made them think that there was something gone wrong with him. . . . (18)

The scene produces an effect of eerie suggestiveness, an intimation of the hidden sickness which pervades the world of the story, the "maleficent and sinful being" which the boy has sensed in "the word *paralysis*." The effect is intensified by the tension between this vaguely sensed threat and the banal, awkward understatement through which it emerges. The scene is symbolic in the sense that it presents a realistic situation which conveys suggestions of further significance, but not in the sense that its characters and images can be assigned specific symbolic meanings. This is what is meant by an epiphany.

The idea of the epiphany can thus explain some important characteristics of *Dubliners*: the stories repeatedly move toward the ironic exposure of spiritual deficiency; realistic materials acquire heightened significance from Joyce's selection and organization. The idea can also help to illuminate the characteristic form of the stories. Much of the effect of the scene from "The Sisters" depends on the emphasis it acquires at the story's conclusion. Joyce cuts off his story in the midst of the old woman's speech, terminating it in an ostensibly arbitrary fashion which yet completes its essential disclosure. Implicit here is a conception of form which has little to do with plot or story in any traditional sense. The story is complete, not because it has presented the beginning, middle, and end of a plot, but because it has achieved its epiphany. The same effect of apparent arbitrariness and actual completion may be seen in the conclusion of "Grace," which ends in the midst of Father Purdon's sermon, epiphanizing the sterility of his secularized religion by giving formal emphasis to his commercial

---

forty epiphanies which have survived are used in *Dubliners*, but these apparently represent less than half of the original collection.

metaphor: "—Well, I have looked into my accounts. I find this wrong and this wrong. But with God's grace, I will rectify this and this. I will set right my accounts" (174). Other stories, particularly "The Dead," display more plot, more of a causally structured action, but in every case the form is determined by a pattern of significance which the final moment completes. "The Sisters" and "Grace" end with moments of speech, "Two Gallants" with a gesture; "Araby" and "The Dead" each end in "a memorable phase of the mind itself." The latter sort of epiphany is closer to traditional moments of recognition, in which the protagonist himself experiences the story's revelation. Thus the boy of "Araby" arrives at a moment of self-recognition: "Gazing up into the darkness I saw myself as a creature driven and derided by vanity; and my eyes burned with anguish and anger" (35). Most of the characters of *Dubliners* are incapable of this degree of consciousness, however. Joyce's epiphanies are primarily revelations for the reader, rather than for the characters. From the ironic distance created by his "style of scrupulous meanness," we perceive the significance of their paralyzed lives.

Because the epiphany must appear as an objective revelation rather than a personal interpretation of reality, it requires such distance as part of a general strategy of indirection. Instead of telling us directly about his characters in the manner of many traditional novelists, Joyce makes them betray themselves. Occasionally we do find traditional, omniscient commentary, such as the observation in "The Boarding House" that Mrs. Mooney, the butcher's wife, "dealt with moral problems as a cleaver deals with meat" (63), but such epigrammatic, authorial analysis soon yields to a style which reflects the vulgar, mercenary mind of "the Madam" herself: "She knew he had a good screw [i.e., wage] for one thing and she suspected he had a bit of stuff put by" (65). Joyce's style scrupulously registers the meanness of his subject. His characters also reveal themselves in speech which invites our comic appreciation of its energy at the same time that we ironically perceive its vacuity. A fine example is the dialogue of Mr. Kernan and his friends in the central section of "Grace," as they make a well-meaning muddle of Church history and whiskey. A comparable effect is produced in "Ivy Day in the Committee Room," but the latter story develops a sharper irony through the contrast between the venality of its petty politicians and the heroic figure of the dead Parnell, in whose memory the ivy is worn. "We all respect him now that he's dead and gone," says Mr. O'Connor; only the *"Pok!"* of another cork escaping from a bottle of stout is needed to complete the satiric exposure (132). The end of the story enforces a further distance by its shift into indirect discourse: "Mr. Crofton said that it was a very fine piece of writing" (135). The emotion of Hynes' poem is genuine; only its expression is pathetically, ludicrously inadequate, and it is just this aspect which Mr. Crofton singles out for his insincere praise.

These later stories convey a clear sense of the sympathy which is blended with Joyce's irony. The ending of "The Dead," which is also a synoptic conclusion for the entire collection, focuses these attitudes in the lyrical symbolism of the final paragraph:

> A few light taps upon the pane made him turn to the window. It had begun to snow again. He watched sleepily the flakes, silver and dark, falling obliquely against the lamplight. The time had come for him to set out on his journey westward. Yes, the newspapers were right: snow was general all over Ireland. It was falling on every part of the dark central plain, on the treeless hills, falling softly upon the Bog of Allen and, farther westward, softly falling into the dark mutinous Shannon waves. It was falling, too, upon every part of the lonely churchyard on the hill where Michael Furey lay buried. It lay thickly drifted on the crooked crosses and headstones, on the spears of the little gate, on the barren thorns. His soul swooned slowly as he heard the snow falling faintly through the universe and faintly falling, like the descent of their last end, upon all the living and the dead. (223–24)

Joyce's symbolism maintains a balanced ambiguity whose underlying structure reflects his corresponding balance of judgment and sympathy toward the world of *Dubliners*. The phrase "the time had come for him to set out on his journey westward," for example, invokes the traditional association of west and death, but also draws on the associations it has acquired in the story. Gabriel's earlier rejection of the idea of a vacation trip to the west has marked his alienation from his country and his wife, who comes from western Ireland. The phrase thus suggests a movement both toward death and toward reconciliation. The image of the snow likewise suggests death, or frozen paralysis, but also, as it joins all the parts of Ireland, living and dead, past and present, suggests inclusive sympathy. The passage, with its last words repeating the story's title, extends its implications to the entire world of *Dubliners,* whose inhabitants appear as joined both in a kind of community and a kind of living death. The direct personal expression of these attitudes could only reveal Joyce's mixed feelings about his city, but distanced and objectified by his artistic indirection those feelings are transformed into a moment of impersonal aesthetic equilibrium.

Although the emergence of this complex moral attitude at the conclusion of *Dubliners* qualifies the harsher irony of the earlier stories, it also expresses a meaning which is implicit from the beginning. In January, 1904, several months before Joyce began the stories of *Dubliners,* he wrote a brief "Portrait of the Artist," in which, at the moment of crucial recognition, the autobiographical artist-hero recalls the words of St. Augustine: "It was manifested unto me that those things be good which yet are corrupted; which neither if they were supremely good, nor unless they were good could be corrupted." [21] The stories of *Dubliners* may emphasize corruption, but they also acknowledge the good which it necessarily implies. Paralysis implies prior vitality, whose memory takes the form of haunting presences, such as the ghosts of Parnell or Michael Furey. The sterile alienation of Gabriel Conroy, like that of the boys in the first three stories or Mr. Duffy in "A Painful Case," is exposed as an inadequate response to Irish paralysis. The possibility of new life depends on the recognition of value in the diseased world of Dublin, as well as the recognition of its sickness. Such respect for the corrupted goodness of the actual world is also implied in the aesthetic of the epiphany, a method which creates significance extending beyond the literal, naturalistic level and yet preserves contact with it; which does not completely subordinate the concrete particular to general symbolic patterns. The ironic exposure of the epiphany anatomizes but does not annihilate its subject.

The method and form of these stories—their characteristic movement toward static moments of apprehension and the equipoise of detachment and sympathy—may thus be seen as the result of Joyce's conception of the epiphany. As Theodore Spencer has observed, such a conception "implies a lyrical rather than a dramatic view of life. It emphasizes the radiance, the effulgence, of the thing itself revealed in a special moment, an unmoving moment of time." [22] In Joyce's artistic development, the period in which he was primarily concerned with recording his epiphanies was one of transition from lyric poetry to prose fiction; the stories of *Dubliners* are closer in form to the lyric than to the traditional novel. Yet their materials are those of a resolute naturalism, the commonplace occurrences of urban life. Joyce's distinctive achievement in *Dubliners* is his synthesis of such form and such content, his ability to create, by the implications of selection and presentation, a larger significance for his fictional world. Despite the disagreement of Joyce's critics over the nature of this significance and the way it is produced, all now recognize that it extends beyond the literal level of his stories.

[21] *The Workshop of Daedalus,* p. 65.

[22] Introduction to *Stephen Hero,* ed. Theodore Spencer (New York: New Directions Publishing Corporation, 1944), p. 17. Copyright © 1944 by New Directions Publishing Corporation. Reprinted by permission of New Directions Publishing Corporation.

V

Joyce's impersonal, indirect manner and his lyrical, epiphany-centered form have by now been assimilated into the tradition of the modern short story. It has become common for writers to locate significance within ordinary experience, to write, in a restrained, economical style, stories which turn on moments of realization rather than dramatic, external events. But we should not allow this familiarity to obscure Joyce's achievement. *Dubliners* is a remarkable work for a writer in his early twenties and in the first decade of the century. It leaves behind the rhetoric of nineteenth-century fiction and concentrates instead on that precise rendering of the object which became the basis of much modern poetry as well as prose.[23] The lesser stories, such as "After the Race" or "A Mother," now have little more than this historical interest. Their place in the larger design of *Dubliners* and the fact that their author went on to become the century's greatest writer of fiction in English are responsible for whatever critical attention they still receive. The major stories—"The Sisters," "Ivy Day in the Committee Room," and, above all, "The Dead"—would in themselves have sufficed to maintain his reputation. Beyond the merits of individual stories, however, there is the achievement of *Dubliners* as a unity, a compound image of the city out of whose shabby reality Joyce wrought not only a chapter of his country's moral history but an important chapter in the history of his art.

[23] See A. Walton Litz, *James Joyce* (New York: Twayne Publishers, Inc., 1966), pp. 50 and 113, for a discussion of the similarities between Joyce's prose and the principles of the Imagist movement in modern poetry, with its insistence on "direct treatment of the THING whether subjective or objective, and the use of NO WORD that does not contribute to the presentation" (the first two principles of the 1912 "Imagist Manifesto").

Work in Progress

by Frank O'Connor

James Joyce is fortunate in having escaped from the necessity of publishing either his collected or selected stories. A good book of stories like a good book of poems is a thing in itself, the summing up of a writer's experience at a given time, and it suffers from being broken up or crowded in with other books. *The Untilled Field, Winesburg, Ohio, England My England, Fishmonger's Fiddle,* and *In Our Time* should be read by themselves, as unities, and preferably in editions that resemble the originals. That is how we have to read *Dubliners,* and its uniqueness is one reason for its continuing reputation.

Joyce has escaped the fate of other storytellers because he gave up writing stories after its publication. Why did he give up? It is typical of the muddle of Joycean criticism in our time that nobody even seems to see the importance of this question, much less tries to answer it. Yet, surely, it is a fairly obvious question. Joyce was a much better storyteller than a poet, but after "Chamber Music" he did not entirely give up lyric poetry, and in fact he improved greatly on his early work. Why did he not write another story after "The Dead"? Is it because he felt that he was not a storyteller or that he believed that he had already done all that could be done with the form? It is as difficult to think of a real storyteller, like Chekhov, who had experienced the thrill of the completed masterpiece, giving up short stories forever as it is to think of Keats giving up lyric poetry. This is a question to which *Dubliners* should suggest an answer, and I am assuming that it does so.

Clearly there is a considerable formal difference between the stories at the beginning of the book and "The Dead" at the end of it, and though they are probably not printed in the strict order of their composition, they illustrate at least four and probably five stages in the development of a storyteller.

The first group of stories are what a magazine editor might legitimately describe as "sketches." The first, "The Sisters," describes two ignorant old sisters of a scholarly priest who has been deprived of his clerical functions because of some sort of nervous breakdown. The point of it still eludes me. There is no doubt about the point of "An Encounter," in which two boys mitching from school meet a sexual "queer." The third describes a small boy who goes late to a fun fair called "Araby" to bring home a present for his favorite girl, the sister of a friend, but arrives just as the fair is closing.

These seem to be all autobiographical fragments from early boyhood and any of them could easily have been included in the autobiographical novel, *A Portrait of the Artist as a Young Man*—that is, if they are not actually fragments from the early draft of this known as *Stephen Hero*. Apart from the very simple Jamesian antithesis in "An Encounter" which, in a more elaborate form, was to become one of Joyce's favorite devices, the stories are interesting mainly for their style. It is a style that originated with Walter Pater but was then modeled very closely on that of Flaubert. It is a highly pictorial style; one intended to exclude the reader from the action and instead to present him with a series of images of the events described, which he may accept or reject but cannot modify to suit his own mood or environment. Understanding, indignation, or compassion, which involve us in the action and make us see it in terms of our own character and experience, are not called for.

> One evening I went into the back drawing-room in which the priest had died. It was a dark, rainy evening and there was no sound in the house. Through one of the broken panes I heard the rain impinge upon the earth, the fine incessant needles of water playing in the sodden beds. Some distant lamp or lighted window gleamed below me.

Or take this, from the same story:

> The high cold empty gloomy rooms liberated me and I went from room to room, singing. From the front window I saw my companions playing below in the street. Their cries reached me weakened and indistinct and, leaning my forehead against the cool glass, I looked over at the dark house where she lived.

"Cool" as an adjective for glass and "dark" as an adjective for house would have been perfectly normal in any other writer of the time, but the two used together like this in the one sentence indicate the born stylist. Every word in these passages is right. Even the lack of punctuation in "the high cold empty gloomy rooms," a combination of adjectives that few writers would have allowed themselves, is calculated, and the combination itself is worked out almost experimentally. Because he is so small, the first thing the boy notices is that the rooms are high; then he perceives the cold and associates it with the rooms themselves; then he realizes that they are cold because they are empty, and finally comes the emotive adjective "gloomy" that describes their total impression. But because the impression is total and immediate there is no punctuation as there is, for instance, in "a dark, rainy evening."

You may play about as you please with alternatives to this phrase; you will find no combination of adjectives that will produce a similar effect, nor any way of reading the passage that will produce a different one. This is using words as they had not been used before in English, except by Pater—not to describe an experience, but so far as possible to duplicate it. Not even perhaps to duplicate it so much as to replace it by a combination of images—a rhetorician's dream, if you like, but Joyce was a student of rhetoric. And while the description of the experience in Dickens or Trollope would have been intended to involve the reader in it and make him feel as author and character were supposed to feel, the replacement of the experience by a verbal arrangement is intended to leave him free to feel or not, just as he chooses, so long as he recognizes that the experience itself has been fully rendered. The result is that reading a story like "Araby" is less like one's experience of reading than one's experience of glancing through a beautifully illustrated book.

The stories in *Dubliners* were arranged rather in the way a poet arranges lyrics in a book, to follow a pattern that exists in his own mind, but, as I have said, there is also a clear chronological pattern, and in the middle of the book is a group of stories that must have been written after "The Sisters" and before "The Dead." These are very harsh naturalistic stories about Dublin middle-class life either in the form of mock-heroic comedy or in that of antithesis. In the former are stories like "Two Gallants," which describes with intense gravity the comic anxiety of two wasters as to whether one of them will be able to extract some money from the little servant girl who is his mistress, and "Clay," which describes an old maid who works in a laundry and the succession of utterly minor disasters that threatens to ruin her celebration of Halloween in the home of her married nephew. In the latter group are "Counterparts," in which a drunken Dublin clerk who has been publicly tongue-lashed by his employer takes it out in the flogging of his wretched little boy who has allowed the fire to go out, and "A Little Cloud," in which an unsuccessful poet is confronted by a successful journalist who has had sense enough to clear out of Dublin in time. They are ugly little stories, however you regard them, but in their re-creation of a whole submerged population they prove that Joyce was at the time a genuine storyteller with a unique personal vision.

It is even more important to notice that in these stories there is also a development of the stylistic devices one finds in the early stories. In *The Mirror in the Roadway* I have already analyzed the first paragraph of "Two Gallants," but it is necessary to consider it here as well.

> The grey warm evening of August had descended upon the city and a mild warm air, a memory of summer, circulated in the streets. The streets, shuttered for the repose of Sunday, swarmed with a gaily coloured crowd. Like illumined pearls the lamps shone from the summits of their tall poles upon the living texture below which, changing shape and hue unceasingly, sent up into the warm grey evening air an unchanging, unceasing murmur.

In this beautiful paragraph we find a remarkable development of the prose style in the earlier stories. Not only are adjectives selected with finicking care ("tall poles"), but some of the words are being deliberately repeated, usually in a slightly different order and sometimes in a slightly different form to avoid giving the reader the effect of mere repetition and yet sustain in his mind the hypnotic effect of repetition. One of the ways in which this is done is by the repetition of a noun at the end of one sentence as the subject of the following sentence—"streets. The streets—" but the key words are "warm," "grey," "unchanging," and "unceasing." The same device is used in another paragraph of the same story, which describes a harpist in Kildare Street.

> He plucked at the wires heedlessly, glancing quickly from time to time at the face of each new-comer and from time to time, wearily also, at the sky. His harp, too, heedless that her coverings had fallen about her knees, seemed weary alike of the eyes of strangers and of her master's hands. One hand played in the bass the melody of *Silent, O Moyle,* while the other hand careered in the treble after each group of notes. The notes of the air sounded deep and full.

Here, not only is Joyce insisting that we shall see the scene exactly as he saw it by his use of Flaubert's "proper word," he is insisting that we shall *feel* it as he felt it by a deliberate though carefully concealed juxtaposition of key words like "heedless," "hand," "weary," and "notes." This sort of incantatory writing is something entirely new in English prose, whether or not it is for the benefit of literature. My own impression, for what it is worth, is that in pictorial writing like the first paragraph, it is absolutely justified, but that when—as in the second paragraph—it expands to the expression of mood it is intolerably self-conscious. The personification of the harp as a woman, naked and weary of men's fumbling fingers, reminds me somewhat of the fat beginning to congeal about an otherwise excellent mutton chop. In literature certain dishes are best served cold—and these may

be taken to include all material descriptions; others that have to do
with passion and mood should come to us piping hot.

The most interesting of these stories are what I assume to be the
final group—"Ivy Day in the Committee Room," "Grace," and "The
Dead," though the last named might very properly be regarded as
belonging to a different type of story again. The first two are in the
mock-heroic manner, one dealing with Irish politics after Parnell, the
other with Irish Catholicism. In "Ivy Day" a group of canvassers and
hangers-on of a local government election are gathered in the cheer-
less headquarters of the Nationalist candidate, waiting to be paid, or
at least hoping for a bottle of stout from the candidate's publichouse.
A Parnellite drops in and departs, and Mr. Henchy, the most talkative
of the group, suggests that his devotion to Parnell is suspect and that
he may even be a British spy. Then the boy arrives with the bottles of
stout, the party cheers up, and when Joe Hynes, the Parnellite, returns he is greeted quite warmly—Mr. Henchy even calling him "Joe,"
a device that we later find, greatly magnified, in *Ulysses*. Three corks,
removed by the old-fashioned method of heating the bottles, pop one
after another, and Joe recites his reach-me-down lament for the dead
Chief. As I have pointed out elsewhere, the three corks represent the
three volleys over the hero's grave and the lament is the pinchbeck
substitute for a Dead March. This is the mock-heroic at its poker-
faced deadliest. In "Two Gallants" the greatest possible demand that
the Irish imagination can make on a woman in love is the gift of a
pound; in "Ivy Day" the greatest tribute a degenerate nation can pay
to a dead leader is the popping of corks from a few bottles of stout,
earned by the betrayal of everything for which that leader had stood.

As I have said, there is no difficulty in imagining the first group of
stories from *Dubliners* transferred to the pages of *A Portrait of the
Artist as a Young Man*. Can one imagine "Ivy Day" transferred to
them? In the Christmas Day scene in that book we have the subject of
"Ivy Day" but treated with almost hysterical violence; and it is as
impossible to imagine transferring "Ivy Day" to that context as it is to
imagine *Dubliners* with the Christmas Day scene in place of "Ivy Day
in the Committee Room." Already as a storyteller Joyce has reached
a parting of the ways; he has excluded certain material from his
stories. In doing so, he has made a mistake that is fatal to the storyteller. He has deprived his submerged population of autonomy.

This sounds more difficult than it really is. A storyteller may make
his submerged population believe and say outrageous things—that is
partly what makes them a submerged population. Gorky's tramps,
Chekhov's peasants, Leskov's artisans, believe things that would drive
an ordinary schoolchild to hysterics, but this does not mean that they

are not intellectually our equals and better. They have skill and wisdom of their own.

This is what the characters in "Grace" do not have. In this story we see the majesty of the Catholic Church as it appears when reflected in the Dublin lower middle classes. According to Joyce's brother, Stanislaus, the story is based on the theme of the *Divine Comedy*, beginning in Hell—the underground lavatory of a publichouse; ascending to Purgatory—the sickbed of a suburban home; and finally to Heaven in Gardiner Street Church. This is likely enough, because Joyce was an intensely literary man, and—in his later work at least—loved to play the well-known literary game of basing his books on underlying myths and theories so that half the reader's fun comes of spotting the allusions—a game which has the incidental advantage that the flattered reader is liable to mistake the author for a literary scholar.

When we first meet him, Mr. Kernan, the commercial traveler, has fallen down the stairs to the lavatory of a publichouse, and lies there unconscious with a portion of his tongue bitten off. The temporal power, in the person of a policeman, appears, ready to lead him to the bridewell, but he is rescued by a Mr. Power, who brings him home instead. Mr. Kernan's friends decide that for the good of his soul he must join them in a retreat, so they gather about his bedside—Mr. Cunningham, Mr. Power, Mr. M'Coy, and Mr. Fogarty. They discuss first the temporal power in the shape of the policeman who had all but arrested Mr. Kernan—a scandalous business, as they agree; and then the spiritual power in terms of all the churchmen they have known or heard of—heard of, one must admit, at some considerable distance, for the whole discussion is on the level of folklore.

Finally, the four men with their penitent friend attend Gardiner Street Church, where they hear a sermon from the eminent Jesuit, Father Purdon. Father Purdon preaches on what he admits is a difficult text—"Wherefore make unto yourselves friends out of the mammon of iniquity so that when you die they may receive you into everlasting dwellings." Father Purdon assumes it to be "a text for business men and professional men," but, whatever it may be, it is quite clear that Father Purdon knows precisely as much about it as Mr. Cunningham does about church history, which is sweet damn all.

> "I often heard he [Leo XIII] was one of the most intellectual men in Europe," said Mr. Power. "I mean, apart from his being Pope."
>
> "So he was," said Mr. Cunningham, "if not *the* most so. His motto, you know, as Pope, was *Lux upon Lux*—*Light upon Light*."
>
> "No, no," said Mr. Fogarty eagerly. "I think you're wrong there. It was *Lux in Tenebris,* I think—*Light in Darkness*."

"O yes," said Mr. M'Coy, "*Tenebrae.*"

"Allow me," said Mr. Cunningham positively, "it was *Lux upon Lux.*
And Pius IX his predecessor's motto was *Crux upon Crux*—that is *Cross
upon Cross*—to show the difference between their two pontificates."

Joyce, the ecclesiastical scholar, the all-but-Jesuit, is in a position
to sneer at them all. Gorky, Leskov, or Chekhov would not have
sneered. Joyce's submerged population is no longer being submerged
by circumstances but by Joyce's own irony.

I am sure that Stanislaus Joyce represented truthfully his brother's
description of the significance of the story because it is quite clear
that Mr. Kernan's fall down the lavatory stairs does represent the Fall
of Man. What I am not satisfied of is that Stanislaus was given the full
explanation, because it seems to me equally clear that Mr. Cunningham, Mr. M'Coy, Mr. Fogarty, and Mr. Power represent the Four
Evangelists, though my mind totters at the thought of trying to find
which evangelist each represents and the evangelists' attributes in
their names and characters. I do not understand the elaborate antithesis of spiritual and temporal powers, or the discussion of the good and
bad types in each, but it seems clear to me that this is the biblical
story, told in terms of the Dublin middle classes and reduced to farce
by them as the story of the Hero is reduced to farce by them in "Ivy
Day in the Committee Room."

"The Dead," Joyce's last story, is entirely different from all the
others. It is also immensely more complicated, and it is not always
easy to see what any particular episode represents, though it is only
too easy to see that it represents something. The scene is the annual
dance of the Misses Morkan, old music teachers on Usher's Island, and
ostensibly it is no more than a report of what happened at it, except
at the end, when Gabriel Conroy and his wife Gretta return to their
hotel room. There she breaks down and tells him of a youthful and
innocent love affair between herself and a boy of seventeen in Galway,
who had caught his death of cold from standing under her bedroom
window. But this final scene is irrelevant only in appearance, for in
effect it is the real story, and everything that has led up to it has been
simply an enormously expanded introduction, a series of themes all
of which find their climax in the hotel bedroom.

The setting of the story in a warm, vivacious lighted house in the
midst of night and snow is an image of life itself, but every incident,
almost every speech, has a crack in it through which we perceive the
presence of death all about us, as when Gabriel says that Gretta "takes
three *mortal* hours to dress herself," and the aunts say that she must
be "perished alive"—an Irishism that ingeniously suggests both life

and death. Several times the warmth and gaiety give rise to the idea of love and marriage, but each time it is knocked dead by phrase or incident. At the very opening of the story Gabriel suggests to the servant girl, Lily, that they will soon be attending her wedding, but she retorts savagely that "the men that is now is only all palaver and what they can get out of you," the major theme of the story, for all grace is with the dead: the younger generation have not the generosity of the two old sisters, the younger singers (Caruso, for instance!) cannot sing as well as some long dead English tenor. Gabriel's aunt actually sings "Arrayed for the Bridal," but she is only an old woman who has been dismissed from her position in the local church choir.

Gabriel himself is fired by passion for his wife, but when they return to their hotel bedroom the electric light has failed, and his passion is also extinguished when she tells him the story of her love for a dead boy. Whether it is Gabriel's quarrel with Miss Ivors, who wants him to spend his summer holiday patriotically in the West of Ireland (where his wife and the young man had met), the discussion of Cistercian monks who are supposed to sleep in their coffins, "to remind them of their last end," or the reminiscences of old singers and old relatives, everything pushes Gabriel toward that ultimate dissolution of identity in which real things disappear from about us, and we are as alone as we shall be on our deathbeds.

But it is easy enough to see from "The Dead" why Joyce gave up storytelling. One of his main passions—the elaboration of style and form—had taken control, and the short story is too tightly knit to permit expansion like this. And—what is much more important—it is quite clear from "The Dead" that he had already begun to lose sight of the submerged population that was his original subject. There are little touches of it here and there, as in the sketches of Freddy Malins and his mother—the old lady who finds everything "beautiful"— "beautiful crossing," "beautiful house," "beautiful scenery," "beautiful fish"—but Gabriel does not belong to it, nor does Gretta nor Miss Ivors. They are not characters but personalities, and Joyce would never again be able to deal with characters, people whose identity is determined by their circumstances. His own escape to Trieste, with its enlargement of his own sense of identity, had caused them to fade from his mind or—to put it more precisely—had caused them to reappear in entirely different guises. This is something that is always liable to happen to the provincial storyteller when you put him into a cosmopolitan atmosphere, and we shall see something of the same kind happening to D. H. Lawrence and A. E. Coppard, not always, as I hope my readers will understand, to our loss or theirs.

I have no doubt that if we possessed the manuscript of the short story that Joyce called "Mr. Hunter's Day" and which was written as

one of the *Dubliners* group, we should see that process actually at
work because it later became *Ulysses.* I assume that it was written
in the manner of "Grace" and "Ivy Day in the Committee Room" as
a mock-heroic description of a day in the life of a Dublin salesman
like Mr. Kernan, with all its petty disasters and triumphs, and would
guess that it ended exultantly with an order for twenty pounds' worth
of hardware or office equipment. But Mr. Bloom in *Ulysses* is no Mr.
Hunter. He is not a member of any submerged population, Irish or
Jewish, whose character could be repressed by the loss of a few orders.
Mr. Bloom has lost orders before this. He is a man of universal in-
telligence, capable of meditating quite lucidly, if irregularly, on an
enormous variety of subjects. In fact, he is Ulysses, and can achieve
anything his great precursor achieved. As for his wayward wife, she
is not only Penelope but Earth itself, and her lover, Blazes Boylan, is
the Sun, which is forever blazing and boiling—why do Joyce commentators always miss the obvious? But what have those colossi to do
with Corley and his pound note and Lenehan and his poor pitiful
plate of peas?

And even these, when translated into the pages of *Ulysses* and
Finnegans Wake have suffered a sea change. They too have resigned
their parts "in the casual comedy." In *Dubliners* Martin Cunningham
may talk of "Lux upon Lux" and "Crux upon Crux," but who, reading of him in the Hades episode in *Ulysses,* can imagine that dignified
figure committing such childish errors?

However they may delight us in their reincarnations, it is clear that
they have nothing to do with the world of the short-storyteller who
must make tragedy out of a plate of peas and a bottle of ginger beer
or the loss of a parcel of fruitcake intended for a Halloween party.
Before such spiritual grandeur as theirs, there is nothing for him to do
but bow himself modestly out.

Dubliners

by David Daiches

The short stories that make up this book have certain common features in aim and technique; they are realistic in a certain sense, and they have a quite extraordinary evenness of tone and texture, the style being that neutral medium which, without in itself showing any signs of emotion or excitement, conveys with quiet adequacy the given story in its proper atmosphere and with its proper implications. Only the last story in the collection, "The Dead," stands apart from the others; here Joyce has done something different—he has presented a story in a way that implies comment, and he has deliberately allowed his style to surrender, as it were, to that comment, so that the level objectivity of the other stories is replaced by a more lyrical quality.

The first three stories are told in the first person, the principle of selection, which determines the choice, organization, and emphasis of the incidents, being provided by the recollected impressions of the narrator. Thus, in "The Sisters" Joyce gives the constituent parts of what, to a sensitive boy, made up (whether actually or not is irrelevant) a single and memorable experience; and these parts are arranged and patterned in such a way as to give a sense of the unity of the experience to the reader. And although it is irrelevant to the critic whether the events actually occurred or not, it is very relevant that the pattern of events should be one which produces a recognizable experience with its attendant atmosphere. A purely "formal" analysis of any of these stories would be useful—in fact, indispensable—in an endeavor to assess their value as literature, but such an analysis is only the first step in a process; it is not in itself able to tell us why that particular arrangement of incident and description constitutes a totality which has more value than a mere symmetrical pattern or intriguing design. The arrangement of events in "The Sisters" or "Araby" produces a good short story because the result is not merely a pattern *qua* pattern (such has no *necessary* value in literature), but a pattern

"Dubliners." *From* The Novel and the Modern World *by David Daiches (Chicago: The University of Chicago Press, 1960), pp. 66–82. Copyright © 1960 by The University of Chicago Press. Reprinted by permission of the publisher.*

which corresponds to something in experience. For those who, owing
to the circumstances of their life or the limitations of their sensibility,
are unable to recognize that correspondence, the story loses most of its
worth: there is always this limitation to the universality of great literature, this stumbling-block to the purely formal critical approach. A
study of *Dubliners* can tell us a great deal about the function of
pattern in fiction and about the relation between realism as a technique and as an end. No English short-story writer has built up his
design, has related the parts to the preconceived whole, more carefully
than Joyce has done in stories such as "The Sisters," "Two Gallants,"
or "Ivy Day in the Committee Room." Observation is the tool of
imagination, and imagination is that which can see potential significance in the most casual seeming events. It is the more specifically and
consciously artistic faculty that organizes, arranges, balances emphases,
and sets going undercurrents of symbolic comment, until that potential
significance has become actual.

In the second of these stories, "An Encounter," the organizing and
selecting principle is again the boy's impressionable mind and memory
as recalled or conceived by Joyce. It is worth noting how Joyce sets the
pattern going in this and other stories. Descriptive comment concerning the chief characters constitutes the opening paragraph—comment
that wanders to and fro in its tenses, not starting with a clear edge of
incident but with a jagged line, as though memory were gradually
searching out those events which really were the beginning of the design which is a totality in the retrospective mind. Similarly, in "The
Sisters," the opening paragraph consists of an almost regular alterna-
tion of imperfect and pluperfect tenses:

> Night after night I had passed the house . . . and studied the lighted
> square of window. . . . If he was dead, I thought, I would see the
> reflection of candles on the darkened blind. . . . He had often said to
> me: "I am not long for this world," and I had thought his words idle.
> Now I knew they were true. . . .*

These deliberately wavering beginnings serve a double function.
First, they give the author an opportunity of presenting to the reader
any preliminary information that is necessary to his understanding of
the story; they enable him, too, to let out those pieces of information
in the order which will give them most significance and throw the
necessary amount of emphasis onto what the author wishes to be

emphasized. Second, on a simple, naturalistic level they give us the pattern of an experience as it actually is to memory or observation. The beginning is vague (the reader should study the evidence of witnesses in reports of court trials to understand how wavering the beginning of a unified experience is to both observer and sufferer), but once under way the jagged line becomes straight, until the end, which is precise and definite. Our own memories of experiences which have been significant for us will provide sufficient comment on this technique. In those stories which are told in the first person, as memories, the jagged-line openings are more conspicuous than in the stories narrated in the third person: Joyce has not done this accidentally.

Very different are the conclusions of the stories. A series of events is recognized as having constituted a totality, a "significant experience," in virtue of its close, not of its opening. The conclusions of these stories are level and precise, the last lines denoting a genuine climax of realization (if told in the first person) or in the pattern of the objective situation (if told in the third). And the pause is genuine. If the reader were taken on five minutes farther he might find the addition unnecessary or silly, but it would not cancel out the effect of the whole story, as the prolongation of the trick conclusions of so many modern short-story writers would. In many of O. Henry's short stories, for example, where the final point is contained in a fraction of a moment sustained in print simply by the author's refusing to go farther, the conclusion is not a genuine one, no real end to a pattern, but simply a piece of wit on the author's part. The stories they tell are not real patterns or wholes but are made to appear so only by the epigrammatic form of the conclusion, and the point would be lost if the author told his readers the succeeding event. Joyce is not in this tradition—he has more respect for his art. His final pauses are as genuine as the final bars of a Beethoven symphony, though not nearly so obvious. The degeneration of the short story—and the short stage play, too—into the extended epigram was a feature of the 1920's and 1930's. Perhaps it is due to some extent to the influence of the curtain stage, where the author is absolved from the necessity of creating a genuine conclusion by the rapid descent of the curtain, cutting off the audience from the stage at a single stroke. The platform stage of the Elizabethans encouraged healthier tendencies: there the end of the pattern had to be real, the pause a real pause, for there was no slick curtain to relieve the writer of his responsibility. Genuine pause does not imply a long-drawn-out conclusion or an uneconomical art: Joyce's endings are subtle and rapid:

"What do you think of that, Crofton," cried Mr. Henchy. "Isn't that fine? What?"
Mr. Crofton said that it was a very fine piece of writing.

Or:

> Gazing up into the darkness I saw myself as a creature driven and derided by vanity; and my eyes burned with anguish and anger.

And there is the immensely subtle and effective ending of "Grace," concluding in the middle of Father Purdon's sermon. The platform-stage ending does not require verbosity or obviousness; it requires only that the last line shall really conclude the pattern; that the reader's pause shall be real and not forced on him by a trick of the author in refusing to say more when there is more to be said.

"Two Gallants," a gray, unexciting incident whose predominant mood is illustrated by the setting—late Sunday evening in a deserted street of Dublin—is one of Joyce's minor triumphs. It is a perfect example of the organization of the casual until, simply by the order and relation of the parts, it becomes significant, not only a sordid incident that happened at a given moment but a symbol of a type of civilization. The arrangement of detail so as to give the utmost density to the narrative is a striking quality here, as it is in "Ivy Day in the Committee Room." Joyce will pause to elaborate the description of a character at a certain point of the story, and it is only by a careful, critical analysis that we appreciate the full effect of having that pause in that place and in no other. Always the location of particularizing detail is such that it suggests the maximum amount of implication. In "Ivy Day in the Committee Room" two features of Joyce's technique are dominant: first, every action is symbolic of the atmosphere he wishes to create, and, second, the pauses for description are carefully arranged and balanced so as to emphasize the symbolic nature of the action. The introduction of candles to light up the bareness of the room at the particular point in the story when Joyce wishes to draw the reader's attention to its bareness is one of many examples:

> A denuded room came into view and the fire lost all its cheerful colour. The walls of the room were bare except for a copy of an election address. In the middle of the room was a small table on which papers were heaped.

A simple enough piece of description, but it has been held back till now and allowed to emerge naturally as a result of the candle incident at a point where the emphasis on bareness, on the loss of the fire's cheerful color, and on the dreary untidiness of the room, gains its maximum effect as regards both structure and atmosphere. Similarly, the manipulation of the Parnell motif in this story shows great skill. It is suggested in the title, but does not break through to the surface of the story until, at a point carefully chosen by Joyce, Mr. Hynes takes off his coat, "displaying, as he did so, an ivy leaf in the

lapel." And henceforth this motif winds in and out until its culmina-
tion in Mr. Hynes's recitation. And no more effective symbol of the
relation between two of the main interests of Dubliners in the beginning of this century has ever been created than in this simple, realistic piece of dialogue and description:

> "This is Parnell's anniversary," said Mr. O'Connor, "and don't let us
> stir up any bad blood. We all respect him now that he's dead and gone—
> even the Conservatives," he added, turning to Mr. Crofton.
>   Pok! The tardy cork flew out of Mr. Crofton's bottle. Mr. Crofton got
> up from his box and went to the fire. As he returned with his capture he
> said in a deep voice:
>   "Our side of the house respects him because he was a gentleman."

The claims of liquor impinge naturally on those of politics, as anyone who has seen a certain section of the Scottish Nationalists at work
in Edinburgh today can well understand. A similar point is made in
Mr. Kernan's remark in "Grace."

> " 'Course he is," said Mr. Kernan, "and a damned decent Orangeman,
> too. We went into Butler's in Moore Street—faith I was genuinely moved,
> tell you the God's truth—and I remember well his very words. *Kernan,*
> he said, *we worship at different altars,* he said, *but our belief is the same.*
> Struck me as very well put."

This time it is religion and liquor that mingle so effortlessly. The
slipping-in of the name of the bar right beside Mr. Kernan's expression of his genuine religious emotion is realistic and convincing in
itself and is also symbolic in that it makes, thus economically, a point
about the Irish character.

Joyce's realism in *Dubliners* is not therefore the casual observation
of the stray photographer, nor is it the piling-up of unrelated details.
All the stories are deliberately and carefully patterned, all have a
density, a fulness of implication, which the even tone of the narrative
by disguising only renders more effective. The almost terrifying calm
of "An Encounter," the aloof recording of "Eveline," the hard clarity
of carefully ordered detail in "After the Race," the carefully balanced
interiors in "A Little Cloud," the penetrating climax of "Counterparts," the quiet effectiveness of "Clay"—to select only some of the
more obvious points—are the work of an artist whose gift of observation, tremendous as it is, is never allowed to thwart his literary crafts-
manship—his ability to construct, arrange, organize. The two most
impressive stories in the collection are "Ivy Day in the Committee
Room" and the concluding story, "The Dead." The former has in a
high degree all the qualities we have noted; it is as careful a piece of
patterned realism as any writer has given us. But "The Dead" differs

both in theme and technique from all the other stories in *Dubliners* and deserves some discussion to itself.

In "The Dead" Joyce uses a much more expansive technique than he does elsewhere in *Dubliners*. He is not here merely concerned with shaping a series of events into a unity; he has a specific point to make —a preconceived theme in terms of which the events in "The Dead" are selected and arranged. In the other stories there is no point other than the pattern that emerges from his telling of the story; no argument can be isolated and discussed as the "theme" of the story, for the story is the theme and the theme is the story. The insight of the artist organizes the data provided by observation into a totality, but no external principle determines that organization; the principle of organization is determined simply by further contemplation of the data themselves. But "The Dead" is the working-out, in terms of realistic narrative, of a preconceived theme, and that theme is a man's withdrawal into the circle of his own egotism, a number of external factors trying progressively to break down the walls of that circle, and those walls being finally broken down by the culminating assault on his egotism coming simultaneously from without, as an incident affecting him, and from within, as an increase of understanding. Only when we have appreciated this theme does the organization of the story become intelligible to us. On the surface it is the story of Gabriel returning from a jolly time at a party given by his aunts in a mood of desire for his wife and the frustration of that desire on his learning that a song sung by one of the guests at the party had reminded his wife of a youth who had been in love with her many years ago and who had died of pneumonia caught through standing outside her window in the cold and the rain; so that his wife is thinking of that past, in which Gabriel had no share, when he was expecting her to be giving herself to him, the final result being that Gabriel loses his mood of desire and falls asleep in a mood of almost impersonal understanding. But about three-quarters of the story is taken up with a vivid and detailed account of the party, and on first reading the story we are puzzled to know why Joyce devotes so much care and space to the party if the ending is to be simply Gabriel's change of mood on learning how his wife is really feeling. As a piece of simple patterning the story seems lopsided; we have to discover the central theme before we realize how perfectly proportioned the story is.

The theme of the story is the assault on the walled circle of Gabriel's egotism. The first character we see is Lily, the caretaker's daughter, rushed almost off her feet in the performance of her various duties. Then comes a pause, and Joyce turns to describe the Misses Morkan, who are giving the party, and the nature of the function. Then, when this retrospect had been brought up to the time of the opening of the story, Gabriel and his wife enter—late for the party, everyone expecting them. The external environment is drawn first before Gabriel enters and makes it merely an environment for himself. Lily is an independent personality, quite outside Gabriel's environment; she is introduced before Gabriel in order that when Gabriel arrives the reader should be able to feel the contrast between the environment as Gabriel feels it to be (a purely personal one), and as it is to a quite objective observer—the caretaker's daughter to whom the party is just an increase of work. Gabriel is greeted as he enters with a great deal of fuss; he enters naturally into the environment his aunts are preparing for him, but immediately after the greeting he has an illuminating encounter with Lily. He patronizes her, as he had known her since she was a child. He remarks gaily that one of these days he will be going to her wedding. Lily resents the remark and replies bitterly that "the men that is now is only all palaver and what they can get out of you."

What part does this little incident play in the story? It is the first attempt to break down the circle of Gabriel's egotism. He has questioned Lily, not with any sincere desire to learn about her, but in order to indulge his own expansive mood. He does not recognize that Lily and her world exist in their own right; to him they are merely themes for his genial conversation. Gabriel colors at Lily's reply; his egotism is hurt ever so slightly, but the fortress is still very far from taken. How slight the breach was is illustrated by his subsequent action—he thrusts a coin into the girl's hand, warming himself in the glow of his own generosity and not concerned with finding a method of giving that will obviate any embarrassment on Lily's part. On thinking over his encounter with Lily he sees it simply as a failure on his part to take up the right tone, and this failure of his own hurts his pride a little and makes him wonder whether he ought not to change the speech he has prepared for after dinner—perhaps that is the wrong tone too. He sees the whole incident from a purely egotistical point of view; Lily exists only as an excuse for his gesturing, and he is worried lest his gestures are not those which will get most appreciation from his audience.

Then we have Gabriel again in his relation with his aunts. He was always their favorite nephew, we are told. We see his possessive attitude to Gretta, his wife. We see him patting his tie reassuringly when his wife shows a tendency to laugh at him. When that tendency is manifested by Aunt Julia as well he shows signs of anger, and tactful Aunt Kate changes the conversation. The picture of Gabriel as withdrawn behind the walls of his own egotism is carefully built up.

The second assault on Gabriel's egotism is made by Miss Ivors, the Irish Nationalist, who attacks his individualism and asks what he is doing for his people and his country. She succeeds in making Gabriel very uncomfortable, and when she leaves him he tries to banish all thought of the conversation from his memory with the reflection that "of course the girl, or woman, or whatever she was, was an enthusiast but there was a time for all things." He goes on to reflect that "she had tried to make him ridiculous before people, heckling him and staring at him with her rabbit's eyes." And so fails the second attempt to break down the circle of Gabriel's egotism.

Then we see Gabriel in a more congenial atmosphere, where his egotism is safe. He is asked to carve the goose—as usual. But Gabriel has been upset, and his cold refusal of a request by Gretta shows his egotism on the defensive. He runs over the heads of his speech in his mind. It must be changed—changed in such a way as to squash these assaults that are being made on his ego. And so he thinks up a nice, cozy talk about hospitality and humor and humanity and the virtues of the older generation (with which, as against the generation represented by Miss Ivors, he temporarily identifies himself). Eventually the meal begins, and Gabriel takes his seat at the head of the table, thoroughly at ease at last.

Mr. Bartell D'Arcy is Gabriel's counterpart—a figure merely sketched, to serve the part of a symbol in the story. There is deliberate irony on Joyce's part in making Gretta refer to him as conceited in an early conversation with Gabriel. When at dinner a group of guests are discussing with their hostesses the singers of Ireland, their complacency is such as to dismiss Caruso almost with contempt: they had hardly heard of him. Only D'Arcy suggests that Caruso might be better than any of the singers mentioned, and his suggestion is met with skepticism. D'Arcy alone of the guests refuses to drink either port or sherry until persuaded by nudges and whispers. And it is D'Arcy who sings the song that removes Gretta to another world.

Gabriel's speech takes place as planned, and for some time he revels happily in the little world of which he is the center. The party ends and the guests stand with coats on in the hall, about to take their leave. Gabriel is waiting for Gretta to get ready, and as he and others are waiting the sound of someone playing the piano comes down the hall:

> "Who's playing up there?" asked Gabriel.
> "Nobody. They're all gone."
> "O no, Aunt Kate," said Mary Jane. "Bartell D'Arcy and Miss O'Callaghan aren't gone yet."
> "Someone is fooling at the piano anyhow," said Gabriel.

D'Arcy is first "nobody"; then—and it is significant for the structure of the story that it is Gabriel who says this—he is "fooling at the

piano." While Gabriel, a little disturbed again, is making a final effort to re-establish his full sense of his own importance by telling a
humorous story to the circle in the hall and thus becoming again the
center of attraction, the sound of someone singing comes downstairs,
and Gabriel sees his wife listening, standing near the top of the first
flight "as if she were a symbol of something." D'Arcy stops abruptly
on being discovered (again the contrast with Gabriel) and finally
Gabriel and Gretta set out for the hotel where they are to spend the
night, as it is too far to go home at such an hour.

Then comes the climax, when the fortified circle of Gabriel's egotism is battered down by a series of sharp blows. Just at the moment
of his greatest self-confidence and desire for her, Gretta tells him that
she is thinking about the song D'Arcy had sung. He questions her,
first genially, and then, as he begins to realize the implications of the
song for Gretta, more and more coldly:

> "I am thinking about a person long ago who used to sing that song."
> "And who was the person long ago?" asked Gabriel, smiling.
> "It was a person I used to know in Galway when I was living with my
> grandmother," she said.
> The smile passed away from Gabriel's face. . . . **1466339**

Miss Ivor had talked about Galway; it was one of the symbols of that
world of otherness against which Gabriel had been shutting himself in
all evening. This is the beginning of the final assault. Then Gabriel
learns that the "person" was a young boy that Gretta used to know,
long before she knew him. He had been in love with her, and they used
to go out walking together. With cold irony Gabriel asks whether that
was the reason that Gretta had earlier in the evening expressed a desire
to go to Galway for the summer holidays. When she tells him that the
young man is dead—dying long since, when he was only seventeen—
this line of defense is taken away from Gabriel and he falls back onto
his final line:

> "What was he?" asked Gabriel, still ironically.
> "He was in the gasworks," she said.
> Gabriel felt humiliated by the failure of his irony and by the evocation
> of this figure from the dead, a boy in the gasworks.

Gabriel has no further defenses left. He burns with shame, seeing
himself

> as a ludicrous figure, acting as a pennyboy for his aunts, a nervous, well-
> meaning sentimentalist, orating to vulgarians and idealising his own
> clownish lusts, the pitiable fatuous figure he had caught a glimpse of in
> the mirror. Instinctively he turned his back more to the light lest she
> might see the shame that burned upon his forehead.

The full realization that his wife had all along been dwelling in another world, a world he had never entered and of which he knew
nothing, and the utter failure of his irony to bring his wife back to the
world of which he, Gabriel, was the center, finally broke the walled
circle of his egotism. A dead youth, a mere memory, was the center of
the world in which Gretta had all this while been living. As a result
of this knowledge, and the way it has been conveyed, Gabriel escapes
from himself, as it were, and the rest of the story shows us his expanding consciousness until the point where, dozing off into unconsciousness, he feels a sense of absolute unity, of identity even, with all those
elements which before had been hostile to his ego:

> Generous tears filled Gabriel's eyes. . . . The tears gathered more
> thickly in his eyes and in the partial darkness he imagined he saw the
> form of a young man standing under a dripping tree. . . . His own
> identity was fading out into a grey impalpable world: the solid world
> itself, which these dead had one time reared and lived in, was dissolving
> and dwindling.
>
> A few light taps upon the pane made him turn to the window. It had
> begun to snow again. He watched sleepily the flakes, silver and dark,
> falling obliquely against the lamplight. The time had come for him to
> set out on his journey westward. Yes, the newspapers were right: snow
> was general all over Ireland. It was falling on every part of the dark cen-
> tral plain, on the treeless hills, falling softly upon the bog of Allen and,
> further westward, softly falling into the dark mutinous Shannon waves.
> It was falling, too, upon every part of the lonely churchyard where
> Michael Furey lay buried. It lay thickly drifted on the crooked crosses and
> headstones, on the spears of the little gate, on the barren thorns. His soul
> swooned slowly as he heard the snow falling faintly through the universe
> and faintly falling, like the descent of their last end, upon all the living
> and the dead.

The snow, which falls indifferently upon all things, covering them
with a neutral whiteness and erasing all their differentiating details,
is the symbol of Gabriel's new sense of identity with the world, of the
breakdown of the circle of his egotism to allow him to become for the
moment not a man different from all other men living in a world of
which he alone is the center but a willing part of the general flux
of things. The assault, which progressed through so many stages
until its final successful stage, had this result, and the contrast with
the normal Gabriel is complete.

It is only as a result of some such analysis that the organization and
structure of "The Dead" can be seen to be not only effective but in-
evitable. It is a story which, in the elaborateness of its technique and
variations of its prose style (the cadenced inversions of the final passage
form a deliberate contrast with the style of the earlier descriptions,
adding their share to the presentation of the main theme), stands apart

from the others in *Dubliners*. Joyce's versatility is already apparent. "Ivy Day in the Committee Room" has the texture of a Katherine Mansfield story but with a firmness of outline and presentation that Katherine Mansfield lacked in all but two or three of her works. "The Dead" is in a more traditional style, but done with a subtlety and a virtuosity that makes it one of the most remarkable short stories of the present century.

"The Dead" was not part of the original draft of *Dubliners*. It was added later, at a time when Joyce was becoming increasingly preoccupied with the problem of aesthetics. The story is, indeed, a symbolic statement of the aesthetic attitude that he came to accept. Gabriel moves from an egocentric to an impersonal point of view just as the artist (according to Joyce's explanation in *A Portrait of the Artist as a Young Man*) moves from the personal lyrical method to the impersonal dramatic approach. The indifferent acceptance of life as something revolving not round the artist's ego but on its independent axis is for Joyce the ideal aesthetic attitude. Thus "The Dead" is, in some sense, a fable illustrating Joyce's view of the nature of the artist's attitude. It reflects his preoccupation with the problem of defining the aesthetic point of view at this period.

Dubliners

by Hugh Kenner

. . . never dented an idea for a phrase's sake. . . .
Ezra Pound

About 1905 Joyce wrote most of *Dubliners,* a whole which he conceived, with remarkable originality, less as a sequence of stories than as a kind of multi-faceted novel.

He wrote to a prospective publisher:

> I do not think that any writer has yet presented Dublin to the world. It has been a capital of Europe for thousands of years, it is supposed to be the second city of the British Empire and it is nearly three times as big as Venice. Moreover, on account of many circumstances which I cannot detail here, the expression Dubliner seems to me to bear some meaning and I doubt whether the same can be said for such words as "Londoner" and "Parisian". . . .[1]

Dublin is not, that is, an agglomeration of residents, but a city. In its present paralysis, it remains a ghost, not a heap of bones: the ghost of the great conception of the City which polarizes the mind of Europe from the time of Pericles to that of Dr. Johnson. Mr. Eliot saw London as "a heap of broken images"; Joyce's Dublin had none of the random quality characterized by "heap." It was a shell of grandeur populated by wraiths. The *integritas* of the aesthetic image corresponds to something still at a minimal level of organization vitally present in the object of contemplation; but it isn't the sort of organization that fuses in a single action or demands a single narrative. This image Joyce fragmented along its inherent lines of cleavage, the parts he disposed to afford one another the maximum of reinforcement. . . .

> My intention was to write a chapter of the moral history of my country, and I chose Dublin for the scene because that city seemed to me the centre of paralysis. I have tried to present it to the indifferent public under four of its aspects: childhood, adolescence, maturity, and public

"Dubliners." *From* Dublin's Joyce *by Hugh Kenner (London: Chatto & Windus Ltd.; Bloomington, Ind.: Indiana University Press, 1956), pp. 48–68. Reprinted by permission of the publishers.*

[1] Herbert Gorman, *James Joyce* (New York, 1940), V–iv.

life. The stories are arranged in this order. I have written it for the most
part in a style of scrupulous meanness and with the conviction that he is
a very bold man who dares to alter in the presentment, still more to de-
form, whatever he has seen and heard . . .[2]

It is not a sort of photography that the last clause recommends. The
precise locutions, gestures, and things out of which the aesthetic image
is being synthesized must not be "dented for a phrase's sake" nor reduced to accessory status as bits of "local colour" subserving a concep-
tual simplification of their meaning. "The artist who could disentangle
the subtle soul of the image from its mesh of defining circumstances
most exactly and re-embody it in artistic circumstances chosen as the
most exact for its new office, he was the supreme artist." [3]

Polishing the Mirror

The easiest way to isolate the sort of respect for undented verity that
controls these stories is to inspect a few of Joyce's first thoughts. Here
is the à peu près of the ending of "The Boarding House," transcribed
from the fair copy Joyce wrote out on July 1, 1905 (now in the Slocum
collection). The Bovaryste Polly is leaning back on the bed luxuriating
in "secret, amiable memories" while her mother presents the ultimatum
to Mr. Doran down below:

> Her hopes and visions were so intricate that she no longer saw the white
> pillows on which her gaze was fixed or remembered that she was waiting
> for anything. At last she heard her mother calling her and she jumped
> up and ran out to the banisters.
> —Polly! Polly!—
> —Yes, Mamma?—
> —Come down, dear. Mr. Doran wants to speak to you.
> She remembered now what she had been waiting for. This was it.

This is the precarious instant of focus. The story is at that point of
balance where the smallest touch will send its extremes into oscillation.
In these final lines the exact mode of understanding that exists between Polly and her mother is to be revealed, and Polly herself is to be
exactly placed on the scale between narcissism and acumen. "This was
it" implies too crude a prearrangement, and too explicit an awareness
of her own feelings. For the printed text, Joyce deleted it, and made
the last line read simply, "Then she remembered what she had been
waiting for" (69). A few lines earlier, at the point where Polly's reverie
is interrupted, the focus is insufficiently sharp. "Jumped" conveys too

[2] Gorman, V–iv.
[3] *Stephen Hero* (New York, 1955), p. 78.

little. Jumped as at a cue? from vitality? from habit of obedience? And the flat level sentence, its three verbs—"heard," "jumped," "ran"—reduced to equal value, suggests either phases of a continuous action (an unwanted degree of alertness) or a moving continuous with her dreaming (muffling the all-important switch in her level of consciousness). The primary discontinuity Joyce finally indicated by starting a new paragraph. The mode of awakening he defined by substituting for "jumped up," "started to her feet." The secondary discontinuity between the call and the start he rendered by dividing the sentence and deleting the specific "her" as object of "calling." In the printed text, the sentence reads:

> At last she heard her mother calling. She started to her feet and ran to the banisters.

"The Sisters"

Laying hold on the subject, not expressing an attitude to it, sometimes gave Joyce more trouble than such minutiae would imply. One story, the first, "The Sisters," actually got published [4] with the traces of beginner's disdain scarring its paragraphs. Two years later, when the manuscript of the sequence was being put in order, the entire story had to be rewritten to get rid of phrases like "a whimsical kind of providence" and adult cadences like "the ceremonious candles in the light of which the Christian must take his last sleep" (compare the revision—"If he was dead, I thought, I would see the reflection of candles on the darkened blind for I knew that two candles must be set at the head of a corpse"). The "two poor women" reading the death notice were originally "three women of the people." The wonder and the impatience, in the revised version, are placed as those of a boy; in the first draft the boy-persona is an excuse for working in a grown-up commentary of impatience and wonder. The visit to the corpse was originally narrated thus:

> We followed the old woman upstairs and into the dead-room. The room through the lace end of the blind was suffused with dusty golden light amid which the candles seemed like pale thin flames. He had been coffined. Nannie gave the lead and we three knelt down at the foot of the bed. There was no sound in the room for some minutes except the sound of Nannie's muttering, for she prayed noisily. The fancy came to me that the old priest was smiling as he lay there in his coffin.

[4] As "Our Weekly Story" in AE's *Irish Homestead*, August 13, 1904. The quotations here are from Joyce's manuscript in the Slocum collection, which lies between the *Irish Homestead* text and the final version.

Here the priest's smile images nothing more than the narrator's dis-
taste for noisy prayer. In the final version the first sentence of this
becomes half a paragraph, and the prayer-episode itself reads:

> Nannie gave the lead and we three knelt down at the foot of the bed.
> I pretended to pray but I could not gather my thoughts because the old
> woman's mutterings distracted me. I noticed how clumsily her skirt was
> hooked at the back and how the heels of her cloth boots were trodden
> down all to one side. The fancy came to me that the old priest was
> smiling as he lay there in his coffin. (14)*

The shift of the boy's attention from prayer to worn boots is something more than a concretization of "I could not gather my thoughts."
It is of the very essence of the rewritten story. The story balances a
succession of empirical verities—old Cotter's "little beady black eyes,"
"children's bootees and umbrellas," a bowed head scarcely visible above
a banister rail, the worn heel of a boot—against a stirring implication
of maleficent mysteries. Everything that is not of the order of boot-
heels is vague, suggestive, and a little frightening. On the first page the
evenly lighted widow is set against the evil suggestion of the word
"paralysis" ("It sounded to me like the name of some maleficent and
sinful being"). The boy's memories of the dead priest "sitting in his
arm-chair by the fire," the green faded garments, the red handkerchief
blackened with snuff stains, the discoloured teeth, are set against a
current of sinister suggestion: "I felt even annoyed at discovering in
myself a sensation of freedom as if I had been freed from something
by his death."

In the revised text a thematic statement of hopeless paralysis is the
first sentence in the book. The paralysed priest in his arm-chair near
the fire is as Stanislaus Joyce confirms[5] intended as "a symbol of Irish
life, priest-ridden and semi-paralyzed." By presenting the interactions
of this image with the consciousness of a young boy, Joyce introduces at
the outset what was to be the scourge of an older boy in a later book:
"a malevolent reality behind those things I say I fear." [6] The young
boy is a generic Dubliner, or rather the Dubliner is a generic boy, for
whom everything beyond the level of reality represented by boot-heels
is vaguely dangerous: for a grown-up too dangerous to bear thinking
about, though a child may feel the fascination of evil, and if unusually

---

* [All quotations from James Joyce, Dubliners reprinted by permission of The
Viking Press, Inc., Jonathan Cape Limited, The Society of Authors as the literary
representative of the Estate of the late James Joyce, and the Executors of the James
Joyce Estate. Originally published by B. W. Huebsch, Inc., in 1916. All rights
reserved.]

[5] Hudson Review, II–4, 502.
[6] A Portrait of the Artist as a Young Man (New York, 1928), p. 287.

tenacious may grow up capable of recording it. The terrible image on which "The Sisters" closes displays this dimension of Dublin religion exaggerated to a point where it captures the speculation even of adult women:

> ". . . And what do you think but there he was, sitting up by himself in the dark in his confession-box, wide-awake and laughing-like softly to himself?"
>
> She stopped suddenly as if to listen. I too listened; but there was no sound in the house: and I knew that the old priest was lying still in his coffin as we had seen him, solemn and truculent in death, an idle chalice on his breast.
>
> Eliza resumed:
>
> "Wide-awake and laughing-like to himself. . . . So then, of course, when they saw that, that made them think that there was something gone wrong with him. . . ." (18)

This laughter is a dissolution of intolerable tension, as the ego tortured by the strains and responsibilities of mediation with the supernatural retreats into the world of boot-heels and snuff. It is of a piece with the pathic conviviality of the Dublin tavern. "He was too scrupulous always," the sister says; "the duties of the priesthood was too much for him"; and the boy had wondered how anyone ever had the courage to undertake responsibilities so grave as those the priest outlined to him (13). The old man, "too scrupulous always," had attempted to serve the supernatural world on its own terms. Relinquishing that attempt in hysterical laughter, he relapsed into the mode of the less scrupulous everyday priest: moral predicaments became complicated logical questions, the responses of the Mass were pattered through with a boy by rote, the works of the Fathers were "as thick as the *Post Office Directory* and as closely printed as the law notices in the newspaper."

It is the *mechanism* of his paralysed life that needs to be pondered. It offers a complex image of what growing up in Dublin amounted to. The old priest had faced, grappled with, and been bested by the world of mysterious malevolence with which the imagination of the small boy is fascinated. Human kind cannot bear even that much reality. Such as he is will, in a different mode, that boy most probably be: a cheerful habitual inhabitant of the boot-heel world. Such as he is the less scrupulous clergy have always been, though no one calls them mad. He tried, and failed. His paralysis foreshadows that of, say, Father Purdon in "Grace," who without uneasiness speaks the habitual idiom of the business world because he is too coarse-textured ever to have tried:

> But one thing only, he said, he would ask of his hearers. And that was: to be straight and manly with God. If their accounts tallied in every point to say:

"Well, I have verified my accounts. I find all well."

But if, as might happen, there were some discrepancies, to admit the truth, to be frank and say like a man:

"Well, I have looked into my accounts. I find this wrong and this wrong. But, with God's grace, I will rectify this and this. I will set right my accounts." (174)

The Plan: Childhood
("The Sisters"; "An Encounter"; "Araby")

Of Joyce's four divisions, Childhood includes the first three stories, Youth, Maturity, and Public Life four each. These are phases in the onset of the paralysis imaged in "The Sisters"; the final story, "The Dead," exhibits it as a living death. A developing mode of consciousness is carefully controlled throughout the book.

The theme of the two modes of priesthood runs from "The Sisters" through "An Encounter" to "Araby," at which point, with the passing of childhood, the scrupulous and imaginative mode loses its resilience for good. In "An Encounter," Joe Dillon, who used to caper around the garden, "an old tea-cosy on his head, beating a tin with his fist and yelling: 'Ya! yaka, yaka, yaka!' " (19) (like the vested priest at his Latin ritual, or David dancing before the ark) proves to have a vocation for the priesthood: an ebullient young Irishman whom nothing mysterious will much trouble or puzzle. In "Araby," the boy-narrator imagines himself in the streets "bearing his chalice safely through a throng of foes"—as scrupulous as the paralysed Father Flynn, but more cautious; Father Flynn, we remember, broke his chalice. "The Sisters" and "An Encounter," moreover, are linked by father-images. The pervert who interrupts the truant boys' expedition to the Pigeon-house with his talk of whipping "as if he were unfolding some elaborate mystery" (27), and his ambivalent injunctions concerning love (it is by turns natural, a furtive secret, and an occasion for flagellation) is very much like the "malevolent reality" itself: he and Father Flynn exist in a complex relation to one another. And with this man's appearance the mysterious is deflected towards the sexual. In "Araby" the sexual achieves glamorous awakening, and the chalice of youthful confident enterprise is broken against deglamouring inadequacy—the late arrival, the empty bazaar, impractical porcelain vases and flowered tea-sets, two pennies and sixpence. Every kind of frustration is implied in the last two pages of "Araby." The great empty hall is a female symbol, entered at last; and it contains only sparse goods, the clink of money, and tittering banalities.

Nearly all the stalls were closed, and the greater part of the hall was in darkness. I recognized a silence like that which pervades a church after a service. (34)

It was in a dark deserted chapel late at night that Father Flynn had sat in his confession-box laughing softly to himself. The confessional motif gets its final twist:

> Gazing up into the darkness I saw myself as a creature driven and derided by vanity; and my eyes burned with anguish and anger. (35)

The Plan: Adolescence ("Eveline"; "After the Race"; "Two Gallants"; "The Boarding-House")

The next sequence balances two feminine and two masculine modes. Eveline torn between Frank and her father, tugged by the injunction of her dead mother, and reaching at last the automatic decision of inaction, "passive, like a helpless animal"; Polly of the banished father and the unspoken understanding with her mother ("As Polly was very lively the intention was to give her the run of the young men") re-clining after her *geste* with "no longer any perturbation visible on her face" and collaborating in the manoeuvring of the hapless Mr. Doran into her noose: these are the feminine polarities—virgin and temptress —between which all Joyce's women oscillate.

Eveline is the book's second thematic image of paralysis. She is not a protagonist, like Father Flynn, but a mirror. The stress falls less on her intrinsic drabness than on the masculine world (Dublin) in which she is placed and the materials it has given her mind to feed on. It is a choice rather than a judgment that she is called on to make. The substance of the story, her reverie, is entirely in the mode of passion: not a balancing of arguments but the counterposition of the familiar room, the romance surrounding Frank, her father's contrary moods, the music of the distant street-organ.

Between her and the "lively" Polly two male modalities are poised to complete Joyce's generic fourfold pattern. In "After the Race" "life" is imagined as reckless action—Stephen Dedalus' "spell of arms and voices" explicitly geared to the petroleum-reeking Call of the Open Road. "The journey laid a magical finger on the genuine pulse of life and gallantly the machinery of human nerves strove to answer the bounding courses of the swift blue animal" (45): which components are alive in this sentence and which are dead? Zestful technology is shored against Dublin drabness: "At the crest of the hill at Inchicore sightseers had gathered in clumps to watch the cars careering home-ward and through this channel of poverty and inaction the Continent

sped its wealth and industry" (42). "The French, moreover, were vir-
tual victors." Ah, Paris!

Jimmy Doyle, who becomes infatuated with continental swish
and gambles away the patrimony he had intended to invest, is an
avatar of Stephen Dedalus and a Dublin's-eye parody of Jimmy Joyce.
The motor racing, the dress clothes, the dancing on the yacht ("this
was seeing life," 47), the drinking, the wild card games, are all versions
of the anti-Dublin, and that is their attraction for Jimmy. The im-
pecunious artist Villona meanwhile follows their follies, entertains
them, and lets in epiphanic light at the end: "Daybreak, gentlemen!"
(The young Joyce made a few shillings during his first bleak winter in
Paris by interviewing a French motor-racing driver for the *Irish
Times*.)

Jimmy forsaking the "channel of poverty and inaction" for Ségouin's
jet-propelled "life" inverts Eveline's failure to choose life with the
"kindly, manly, openhearted" Frank in Buenos Ayres. The connections
of the second masculine story in the section, "Two Gallants," are with
the second feminine world, the Boarding House of cynical put-up jobs.
Metaphors of prostitution reverberate through both stories: Corley
and Lenehan, achieving at the end of their adventure the small gold
coin, emerge as male street-walkers; as for Mrs. Mooney's Boarding
House, "All the resident young men spoke of her as *The Madam*" (62).

By now the archetypal action of every Joyce work is in full swing.
The gentle lyric antitheses of the first pages are growing sharper, as
the consciousness divided between the public fact and the private
dream incarnates its conflicting elements in the two kinds of men and
two kinds of women who people the epic phase. Later these people
will start meeting one another and realize dimly that they are meeting
themselves.

The Plan: Maturity ("A Little Cloud"; "Counterparts"; "Clay"; "A Painful Case")

The four stories of maturity rearrange the antitheses of the preceding section. This time two masculine worlds are followed by two
feminine ones; more accurately, since the protagonist of "A Painful
Case" is a male clerk, two modes of ethos are followed by two of
pathos.

"A Little Cloud" exhibits the components of "After the Race" in
a more complex context. As Bloom and Dedalus, as Watson and
Holmes, the palefaced Little Chandler encounters the Noble Savage
Gallaher who has Been Abroad and Got On, and by osmosis acquires
a timid share of his virtues. The opposites, as always, belong to the

same species: the feminine Chandler with his "quiet voice" and "refined" manners confronts the *pseudo*-masculine incarnation of irra-
tional know-how. For the first time in the book, the utter absence of
an organic community begins to be insisted on: the "mansions in
which the old nobility of Dublin had roystered" are "spectral" now,
and no memory of the past touches Chandler (71-72). Incommunicable
loneliness has superseded the bravado of adolescence. Chandler has
none of Lenehan's resilience. His shyness prevents his reading the
poetry-books of his bachelor days to his wife: "At times he repeated
lines to himself and this consoled him" (71).

As for Gallaher, his positives are those of the impresario only. The
key-words of the paragraph in which he is first allowed to emerge at
length are tellingly vague. We hear first of "greatness," and the early
sign of that greatness was that people used to say he was "wild." But
nobody denied him "talent." There was "a certain . . . something" in
him that impressed you. Finally it emerges: ". . . he kept up a bold
face" (72).

The osmotic interchange begins in the eighth line of the story: "It
was something to have a friend like that" (70). As he goes off to meet
the anarchic journalist (for that is Gallaher's profession) Chandler
feels "superior to the people he passed" (73). His ambitions rise toward
the Life Literary in emulation: "He wondered whether he could write
a poem to express his idea. . . . He was not sure what idea he wished
to express but the thought that a poetic moment had touched him
took life within him like an infant hope." Communion is achieved
for half a page; the rift begins with Gallaher's patronizing preference
for liquor neat (75), widens through the clash of Chandler's wistful
dream of Europe against Gallaher's reportage, and climaxes with
Chandler's discovery that his prudent marriage earns him no advantage in Gallaher's eyes (81). He remains uneasily pestered (83) by
Gallaher's image of marriage as the poor man's fornication (79), attempts a Gallaherian gesture of "living bravely" by shouting "Stop!"
to the crying child, and subsides into tears of remorse.

Thus the dialectic of "A Little Cloud"; "Counterparts" repeats its
action in a more automatic fashion. The employer's rebuke is exhibited as response-to-stimulus; his fist "seemed to vibrate like the knob
of some electric machine" (91), and his voice in the first sentence of
the story emerges from a speaking-tube. The context of the story is
mechanism. Farrington is a copying-machine geared to a law-machine.
The human cogs and levers of the story whirr and jerk as the rebuke
administered by the employer passes through them and emerges at
the other end as the flailing of a cane on the thighs of a small boy.
In "A Little Cloud" there was no community, only loneliness; in

"Counterparts" there is a pseudo-community of drinking, sterile emulation, action and reaction: a sketch for the monstrous robot body that dominates *Ulysses*.

Maria is "Clay" as humanity itself, as susceptible to moulding, and as death in life. Joe's wife, another Mrs. Mooney, has eased her into the laundry and one may suspect will soon ease her into a convent; and Maria, one is sure, will never quite realize how she got there. The omen she touches is that of death; when she laughs the tip of her nose nearly meets the tip of her chin (101)—like a Hallowe'en witch—and like a banished ghost she returns to Joe's fireside (104), until cockcrow on All Hallow's Eve. The error in her song (106) parallels her recurrent failure to get the ring (101); the song should have gone on to treat of marriage:

> I dreamt that suitors sought my hand
> That knights on bended knee,
> And with vows no maiden heart could withstand
> They pledged their hearts to me.

> And I dreamt that one of that noble band
> Came forth my heart to claim
> But I also dreamt, which charmed me most,
> That you loved me just the same.

The Heart of the Matter: "A Painful Case"

"A Painful Case" occupies the mid-point of the book. It gathers up, specifically, the implications of the third group: Chandler's loneliness, Farrington's automatism (Mr. Duffy "lived at a little distance from his body, regarding his own acts with doubtful side-glances"), Maria's living death. Mr. Duffy is carefully presented for three pages as a person of absolute meticulous voluntary routine. The rare inscribing of sentences in a commonplace-book (held together by a brass pin) is as glamourless an action as is the business of the bank from which at four o'clock daily he is "set free" (108). Passion when it intersects his life proves impossibly circumstanced; he rebukes it; he is touched as by a ghost; and his newly emotionalized mental life (111), brings an eerie ultimate awareness of the loneliness he has until then accepted with his intellect only.

Now that the ghosts have begun to swarm (we are entering the regions of "The Dead") we become aware that it is a living death that the book is presenting. The action of story after story has taken place at night or in twilight; and from "A Little Cloud" to "Ivy Day in the

Committee Room" the season is autumn.[7] "A Painful Case" is the first adumbration of "The Dead": passion missed and returning as the phantom touch of a hand (116), a hallucinatory voice (117), cold air creeping into the sleeves of a coat (116). The malevolent realities surrounding the innocent protagonist of the first part of the book are now part of the texture of life; but the antithesis to the world of boot-heels is no longer the mysterious power that had cracked the mind of its sacerdotal servant: rather, the multiplication of spectres of choices negated, passions unexplored, opportunities missed, aspects of the self denied. The alter ego who returned in the flesh to Little Chandler returns as a wraith to Mr. Duffy.

The theme of might-have-been is endemic to Joyce's books: Richard Rowan's fear lest he deprive his wife of some moments of passion that ought to have been hers, Stephen's speculation ("Weave, weaver of the wind") on the events of history "lodged in the room of the infinite possibilities they have ousted," Anna Livia's disillusion as her Prince Charming's coach dwindles back into a pumpkin: "I thought you were all glittering with the noblest of carriage. You're only a bumpkin. I thought you the great in all things, in guilt and in glory. You're but a puny. Home!" Its layers of meaning are numerous. It is the paralysis of the City, at one level; the rhythm of the Dubliners' lives rises to no festivity and is sustained by no community; in the drabness of mediaeval peasant life without its seasonal joyfulness, they oscillate between bricks and ghosts. It is the paralysis of the person, at another level, though it is seldom evident that these persons are so circumstanced that they might have chosen differently. But at the most important level it is metaphysical: the Exiles are exiled from the garden, and the key to their plight, as *Finnegans Wake* brings forward, is the Fall. Joyce's world, as the Rev. Walter Ong has written of Kafka's, "is governed by the sense in which man's actions are carried on in a setting to which they are irrelevant." [8] Father Ong goes on to define "the great fiction of the West; the self-possessed man in the self-possessed world, the fiction which seeks to erase all sense of plight, of confusing weakness, from man's consciousness, and which above all will never admit such a sense as a principle of operation." Man so constituted, he notes, cannot afford to *give,* since giving recognizes the fact of *otherness,* of a portion of being neither susceptible to his control nor violable to

---

[7] With the exception of "Counterparts," which takes place in a foggy February dusk. The first three stories (Childhood) span the extremes of June and December; the next four (Adolescence) occur in summer (though the time of "Eveline," a bridge from the childhood section—she is nineteen—isn't specified; the street organ suggests summer, however). Autumn follows. With "The Dead" we are plunged into the dead of winter.

[8] Walter J. Ong, S. J., "Kafka's Castle in the West," *Thought,* XXII–86 (Sept. 1947), 439–460.

his gaze; this works out alike between man and man, and between man and God. It is precisely this fiction of self-containment that Joyce defines in successively more elaborate images, from Mr. Duffy's careful control over every detail of life through the tightly-bounded ethical world of *Exiles* and Stephen's "All or not at all" to HCE's solipsistic nightmare. What beats against all these people is the evidence of otherness: the ghosts in *Dubliners*, Richard Rowan's voices on the strand at dawn, Stephen's fear of a "malevolent reality" and his collapse into Dublin itself ("I have much, much to learn"), the voices and tappings that derange Earwicker's slumbers like leaves, twigs, and stones dropped into a pool that craves stagnation.

The focus of Mr. Duffy's plight is achieved in exactly these terms. During his evenings of intellectual friendship with Mrs. Sinico,

> Sometimes he caught himself listening to the sound of his own voice. He thought that in her eyes he would ascend to an angelical stature; and, as he attached the fervent nature of his companion more and more closely to him, he heard the strange impersonal voice which he recognized as his own, insisting on the soul's incurable loneliness. We cannot give ourselves, it said: we are our own. The end of these discourses was that one night during which she had shown every sign of unusual excitement, Mrs. Sinico caught up his hand passionately and pressed it to her cheek. (111)

"Her interpretation of his words disillusioned him." Her touch brings otherness, a world of passion lying outside his controlled and swept and tidied world, a denial of the voice which says "We are our own." The "strange impersonal" quality of that voice is Mr. Duffy's kind of gratuitous illusion, comparable to the dry detachment with which he had translated *Michael Kramer,* the stage directions written in purple ink, trying to pretend that someone else did it, some perfected self disengaged from the tensions of the drama. The voice *is* his own, as Joyce knew and as Duffy himself half recognizes. That is what is unforgivable, that she should challenge his self-sufficiency; and he is thrown off balance, breaks off the affair, and after a false quiet steps into hell.

The Plan: Public Life ("Ivy Day in the Committee Room"; "A Mother"; "Grace")

The public life stories are ampler looks round at the same material, with a shift of emphasis to the social manifestations of self-sufficiency. They enact a muted scherzo between the first climax of the book, Mr. Duffy's contact with the dead and his conviction of haunted aloneness, and the long final epiphany, "The Dead."

In "Ivy Day in the Committee Room" the perspectives of "A Painful Case" begin to expand. The shadow of Parnell to whom they had

made years before the one act of faith of which they were capable lies
over not just one man but a roomful of paralytics. Political activity in
the vacuum left by his departure consists of a few futile gestures,
sporadic interviews with voters, and much meditative drinking of
stout by an October fire. Edward VII, the surrogate father, is the
focus of mild colloquial dissension; the betrayed dead father Parnell
stirs into life through a piece of turgidly sincere declamation: our first
impressive evidence of Joyce's ability to write just the right kind of
bad rhetoric without cynicism. They are the received locutions of
Dublin execrably joined, yet a real grief and loyalty break through.

In "A Mother" factitious culture and gratuitous pride collaborate;
in "Grace," gratuitous friendship and factitious religiosity. The absence in these two stories of the circumambient dead, so insistently
dominant in the preceding three, is not accidental. We are in touch
here with the carapace alone, public life in the boot-heel world. It
is not into the communion of saints that his friends' little plot and
Father Purdon's urbanely muscular sermon induct Mr. Kernan. "If
he might use the metaphor, he said, he was their spiritual accountant"
(174); nothing could make the point more clearly than the presentation
of redeeming spiritual wisdom in two pages of indirect discourse. From
his *selva oscura* at the foot of the lavatory steps, up to the nipping air,
then via a sick bed to a Jesuit Paradiso of "decorous atmosphere" on
Gardiner Street, where his party settles down "in the form of a quincunx" (Dante's courageous made such a cross, in the fifth heaven—*Par.*
XIV)—Mr. Kernan has been led through a Dublin *Commedia*.

> The gentlemen were all well dressed and orderly. The light of the lamps
> of the church fell upon an assembly of black clothes and white collars,
> relieved here and there by tweeds, on dark mottled pillars of green marble
> and on lugubrious canvases. The gentlemen sat in the benches, having
> hitched their trousers slightly above their knees and laid their hats in
> security. They sat well back and gazed formally at the distant speck of
> red light which was suspended before the high altar. (172)

> O abbondante grazia, ond' io presunsi
> ficcar lo viso per la luce eterna
> tanto che la veduta vi consunsi!
>
> *Paradiso* XXXIII, 82–84

When the preacher enters, they produce handkerchiefs, and kneel upon
them "with care."

"A Mother" and "Grace" bring to maximal articulation the world
which the young narrator of "The Sisters" had glimpsed in contem-
plating the untidy hooking of the old woman's skirt and the heels of
her cloth boots trodden down all to one side: that epiphany, we remember, took place at prayer.

The Dead

The motifs of "The Dead" are drawn, in ways we need not detail, from all the stories in the book, but its peculiar modes of consciousness are in touch with "The Sisters" at the beginning and with the "Clay"—"Painful Case"—"Ivy Day" group in the centre. It is towards the definition of living death, as we saw in connection with "Clay," that the entire book is oriented; the first point to grasp about "The Dead" is the universal reference of the title. "I had not thought death had undone so many"; in reading *The Waste Land* aloud Mr. Eliot puts the stress not on "death" but on "undone." The link, through the quotation, with the outer circle of Dante's hell, the souls who lived without blame and without praise, the world of the Hollow Men, is an Eliotic perspective of the utmost relevance to Joyce's story. In "The Dead" everybody is dead. Its Prufrock-world of dinner-parties, elderly aunts, young topers, old lechers, and after-dinner wit ("He ran over the heads of his speech. Irish hospitality, sad memories, the Three Graces, Paris, the quotation from Browning," 192) is summed up in the story of the factory horse that exasperated the fashionable pretensions of its rider by walking round and round the statue of King Billy as around the mill-shaft (208). Music, the subject on which these Dubliners are most articulate, is discussed solely in terms of the good old days (199). And the most living influence in the story is the memory, enclosed in music, of a dead peasant boy.

> We have lingered in the chambers of the sea
> By sea-girls wreathed with seaweed red and brown
> Till human voices wake us, and we drown.*

We drown: "His own identity was fading out into a grey impalpable world: the solid world itself, which these dead had one time reared and lived in, was dissolving and dwindling" (223).

Like the first story in the book, the last presents a world of death dominated by two wraith-like sisters. The priest who had been first deranged, then paralysed, then dead had enacted, we now see in retrospect, a symbolic role of much complexity. The sisters Morkan are custodians of a ritual order, comprising every component of the culture of eighteenth-century Dublin, in whose vitality it is now impossible to

---

* [Quotation from T. S. Eliot, "The Love Song of J. Alfred Prufrock," in *The Complete Poems and Plays, 1909–1950* (New York: Harcourt, Brace & World, Inc.; London: Faber & Faber Ltd., 1950) reprinted by permission of the publishers. Copyright © 1930, 1939, 1943, 1950 by T. S. Eliot and 1934, 1935, 1936, 1952 by Harcourt, Brace & World, Inc.]

feel much faith. It does not, we are made to feel, stand of itself; the being of its world of light, movement, quadrilles, music, and banqueting is sustained, like an underwater bubble, by the pressure of the dark snowy boundlessness outside. Gaiety is oddly unspontaneous, a function of custom, habit, and encouragement:

> A red-faced young woman, dressed in pansy, came into the room, excitedly clapping her hands and crying:
> "Quadrilles! Quadrilles!"
> Close on her heels came Aunt Kate, crying:
> "Two gentlemen and three ladies, Mary Jane!" . . .
> As the piano had twice begun the prelude to the first figure Mary Jane led her recruits quickly from the room. (183–84)

The cultural order has shifted, since Swift's time, from the masculine to the feminine mode. Art is discussed (198) in terms of performers. Creation is unthought of. The world of art is an established order which undergoes the homage of ritual performance. At the same level of triviality, the discussion shifts from art to religion: the pattern of living death emerges:

> He was astonished to hear that the monks never spoke, got up at two in the morning, and slept in their coffins. He asked what they did it for.
> "That's the rule of the order," said Aunt Kate firmly.
> "Yes, but why?" asked Mr. Browne.
> Aunt Kate repeated that it was the rule, that was all. . . . (201)

As for the celebration of artistic mysteries, the respect in which it is surrounded is one of the polite conventions (cf. "the rule of the order") dominated by the Sisters:

> Gabriel could not listen while Mary Jane was playing her Academy piece, full of runs and difficult passages, to the hushed drawing-room. He liked music but the piece she was playing had no melody for him and he doubted whether it had any melody for the other listeners, though they had begged Mary Jane to play something. Four young men, who had come from the refreshment-room to stand in the doorway at the sound of the piano, had gone away quietly in couples after a few minutes. The only persons who seemed to follow the music were Mary Jane herself, her hands racing along the keyboard or lifted from it at the pauses like those of a priestess in momentary imprecation, and Aunt Kate standing at her elbow to turn the page. (186)

The "Academy piece," the departure of the young men "in couples" (moral support for unobtrusive defection), the "priestess" gestures of the performer, the dominating presence of Aunt Kate expediting the mechanism of a culture still in some sense real to her alone, none of these details is accidental. As for male vitality, we have Mr. Browne:

Then he asked one of the young men to move aside, and, taking hold
of the decanter, filled out for himself a goodly measure of whisky. The
young men eyed him respectfully while he took a trial sip.

"God help me," he said, smiling, "it's the doctor's orders."

His wizened face broke into a broader smile, and the three young
ladies laughed in musical echo to his pleasantry, swaying their bodies
to and fro, with nervous jerks of their shoulders. The boldest said:

"O, now, Mr. Browne, I'm sure the doctor never ordered anything of
the kind." (183)

—and Freddy Malins:

Mr. Browne, whose face was once more wrinkling with mirth, poured out
for himself a glass of whisky while Freddy Malins exploded, before he
had well reached the climax of his story, in a kink of high-pitched bron-
chitic laughter and, setting down his untasted and overflowing glass, began to rub the knuckles of his left fist backwards and forwards into his
left eye, repeating words of his last phrase as well as his fit of laughter
would allow him. (185)

We are made to feel the artificially fostered isolation of this merriment in countless insidious ways. Physical separation from Dublin
is implied not only by the frequent references to the cold and dark
out of which the visitors emerge, but by the setting itself, a "dark
gaunt house on Usher's Island, the upper part of which they had
rented from Mr. Fulham, the corn-factor on the ground floor" (176),
which emerges oddly during the scenes of leavetaking as a gaslit oasis
in Limbo. Death is written on the face of Aunt Julia ("Her hair, drawn
low over the tops of her ears, was grey; and grey also, with darker
shadows, was her large flaccid face. Though she was stout in build
and stood erect, her slow eyes and parted lips gave her the appearance
of a woman who did not know where she was or where she was going,"
179) and life on the face of Aunt Kate suggests comparison to "a
shrivelled red apple." Aunt Julia sings Arrayed for the Bridal (193),
and Gabriel catching the haggard look on her face (222) foresees her
death.

It is, significantly, through Gabriel that the anachronistic factitious
quality of the evening's merriment emerges in definitive fashion:

One boot stood upright, its limp upper fallen down: the fellow of it lay
upon its side. He wondered at his riot of emotions of an hour before.
From what had it proceeded? From his aunt's supper, from his own foolish speech, from the wine and dancing, the merrymaking when saying
goodnight in the hall, the pleasure of the walk along the river in the
snow. Poor Aunt Julia! She, too, would soon be a shade with the shade of
Patrick Morkan and his horse. . . . (222)

Gabriel's emotional organization was completed in his youth, in isolation from their world:

> The indelicate clacking of the men's heels and the shuffling of their soles reminded him that their grade of culture differed from his. (179)

—and now in isolation from every context. Boots speak as they did to the boy in "The Sisters." Like Mr. Duffy, Gabriel has constructed about himself an armour of isolation; his own voice speaks to him in countless forms, as it did to Mr. Duffy: "We cannot give ourselves, it said; we are our own" (111). The question, for Gabriel, is only what posture to adopt for minimal friction:

> He would only make himself ridiculous by quoting poetry to them which they could not understand. They would think that he was airing his superior education. He would fail with them just as he had failed with the girl in the pantry. He had taken up a wrong tone. His whole speech was a mistake from first to last, an utter failure. (179)

Lily, the caretaker's daughter, whose pale name is the first word in the story, is only the first of the women who rebuff Gabriel. He is heckled by his wife (180), by his two aunts (181), by Miss Ivors (189); and his wife at the end turns from him for a shade. It is his know-how, chiefly, that commands respect:

> He felt quite at ease now for he was an expert carver and liked nothing better than to find himself at the head of a well-laden table. (197)

Gabriel, then, and the Morkan party are analogous worlds: analogous in their incurable autonomy. He is one closed system. The scheme of values expressed at the annual dance is another. The enveloping background of both is the snow. Gabriel emerges into the house from the snow as from an invigorating medium:

> He continued scraping his feet vigorously while the three women went upstairs, laughing, to the ladies' dressing-room. A light fringe of snow lay like a cape on the shoulders of his overcoat and like toecaps on the toes of his goloshes; and, as the buttons of his overcoat slipped with a squeaking noise through the snow-stiffened frieze, a cold, fragrant air from out-of-doors escaped from crevices and folds. (177)

Their laughter recedes from him; the snow, the "cold, fragrant air," standing for something like Ibsen's envacuumed Norway, is his element. Between his round of infighting with Miss Ivors and the necessities of the dinner-table speech in tribute to the aunts whom he privately reduces to "two ignorant old women" (192), his mind turns to the snow again with longing:

> Gabriel's warm trembling fingers tapped the cold pane of the window. How cool it must be outside! How pleasant it would be to walk out

alone, first along by the river and then through the park! The snow would be lying on the branches of the trees and forming a bright cap on the top of the Wellington Monument. How much more pleasant it would be there than at the supper-table! (192)

The meaning of this desire is clarified much later, when at the beginning of the walk home Gabriel's imagination yields to the passion that is to suffer such deflation in the hotel-room:

Moments of their secret life together burst like stars upon his memory. . . . He was standing with her in the cold, looking in through a grated window at a man making bottles in a roaring furnace. It was very cold. Her face, fragrant in the cold air, was quite close to his; and suddenly he called out to the man at the furnace:
"Is the fire hot, sir?"
But the man could not hear with the noise of the furnace. It was just as well. He might have answered rudely. (213)

The invigorating cold stands for something complexly intrinsic to Gabriel's psychic balance. It is that against which his animal warmth is asserted: an obeisant medium presenting no diplomatic puzzles. And it is the brisk vacant context of his ideal passion for Gretta, once experienced and now remembered, in which they exist alone, in a naked mingling of passions, separated from the ordinary social milieu by a grated window. The picturesque spectacle of the man making bottles in a roaring furnace conveys the spectacular toy-shop quality Dublin acquires when seen from the centre of their union. The snow, ultimately, corresponds to the quality of Gabriel's isolation ("How pleasant it would be to walk out alone by the river and then through the park!"). It is where he feels at home. It is anti-communal; it is that against which the Misses Morkan's Christmas dance asserts warmth and order. Gabriel imagines, as it proves mistakenly, that Gretta has shared it with him. Because it is anti-communal it is death; it triumphs in the end over his soul and, as he foresees, over Aunt Kate and Aunt Julia, and over all Dublin and all Ireland, reducing "the solid world itself, which these dead had one time reared and lived in" to a common level with "the dark central plain," "the bog of Allen," and "the lonely churchyard on the hills where Michael Furey lay buried" (223).

The fragrant air Gabriel had carried into the Misses Morkan's house is the principle of death; it is his proper medium, as he comes to see:

A shameful consciousness of his own person assailed him. He saw himself as a ludicrous figure, acting as a pennyboy for his aunts, a nervous, well-meaning sentimentalist, orating to vulgarians and idealizing his own clownish lusts, the pitiable fatuous fellow he had caught a glimpse of in the mirror. (220)

He and his generation of glib middle-class snobbery and book-reviewing are the exorcism of the ghostly eighteenth-century order that lingers in the salon of his aunts. "Better pass boldly into that other world, in the full glory of some passion," he thinks, "than fade and wither dismally with age" (223). The dancing-party belongs to that which is fading and withering; as for himself, there is no question of passing boldly into that other world. He is already of it. His longing to be alone in the snow was a longing for this death. His soul already pursues the "wayward and flickering existence" of the dead; it has taken very little to cause his identity to fade out "into a grey impalpable world." He is named for the angel who is to blow the last trump; but having released no blast of Judgment he watches through a hotel window the pale flakes falling through darkness.

One of Joyce's Trieste language-pupils recalls him gazing into a glass paperweight of the sort containing floating crystals and murmuring, "Yes, snow is general all over Ireland." Snow continued to fall and Ireland continued to be paralysed, in Joyce's mind, throughout his life.

The Unity of *Dubliners*

by Brewster Ghiselin

The idea is not altogether new that the structure of James Joyce's *Dubliners,* long believed to be loose and episodic, is really unitary. In 1944, Richard Levin and Charles Shattuck made it clear that the book is "something more than a collection of discrete sketches." In their essay "First Flight to Ithaca: A New Reading of Joyce's *Dubliners*," they demonstrated that like the novel *Ulysses* the stories of *Dubliners* are integrated by a pattern of correspondence to the *Odyssey* of Homer. To this first demonstration of a latent structural unity in *Dubliners* must be added the evidence of its even more full integration by means of a symbolic structure so highly organized as to suggest the most subtle elaborations of Joyce's method in his maturity.

So long as *Dubliners* was conceived of only as "a straight work of Naturalistic fiction," the phrase of Edmund Wilson characterizing the book in *Axel's Castle,* its unity could appear to be no more than thematic. The work seemed merely a group of brilliant individual stories arranged in such a way as to develop effectively the import which Joyce himself announced, but did not fully reveal, in describing the book as "a chapter of the moral history of my country" and in suggesting that his interest focused upon Dublin as "the centre of paralysis." As Harry Levin explained in his introduction to *The Portable Joyce,* "The book is not a systematic canvass like *Ulysses*; nor is it integrated, like the *Portrait,* by one intense point of view; but it comprises, as Joyce explained, a series of chapters in the moral history of his community; and the episodes are arranged in careful progression from childhood to maturity, broadening from private to public scope."

So narrow an understanding of *Dubliners* is no longer acceptable. Recent and steadily increasing appreciation of the fact that there is much symbolism in the book has dispelled the notion that it is radi-

"The Unity of Dubliners*" (original title: "The Unity of Joyce's* Dubliners*")* *by Brewster Ghiselin. From* Accent, *XVI (Spring, 1956), 75–88; (Summer, 1956), 196–213. Copyright © 1956 by Brewster Ghiselin. Reprinted by permission of the author.*

cally different in technique from Joyce's later fiction. During the past
six or eight years a significant body of critics, among them Caroline
Gordon, Allen Tate, and W. Y. Tindall, have published their understanding that the naturalism of *Dubliners* is complicated by systematic
use of symbols, which establish relationships between superficially
disparate elements in the stories. Discussion of "The Dead," for example, has made it obvious that the immobility of snowy statues in
that story is symbolically one with the spiritual condition of Gabriel
Conroy turned to the wintry window at the very end of *Dubliners*
and with the deathly arrest of paralysis announced on the first page of
the book. In the light of this insight other elements of the same pattern, such as the stillness of the girl frozen in fear at the end of the
fourth story, virtually declare themselves.

Such images, significantly disposed, give a firm symbolic texture
and pattern to the individual stories of *Dubliners* and enhance the
integrity of the work as a whole. But no constellation, zodiac, or whole
celestial sphere of symbols is enough in itself to establish in the fifteen
separate narratives, each one in its realistic aspect a completely independent action, the embracing and inviolable order of full structural
unity. That is achieved, however, by means of a single development,
essentially of action, organized in complex detail and in a necessary,
meaningful sequence throughout the book. Because this structure is
defined partly by realistic means, partly by symbols, much of it must
remain invisible until the major symbols in which it defines itself are
recognized, as too few of them have been, and displayed in their more
significant relationships. When the outlines of the symbolic pattern
have been grasped, the whole unifying development will be discernible
as a sequence of events in a moral drama, an action of the human spirit
struggling for survival under peculiar conditions of deprivation, enclosed and disabled by a degenerate environment that provides none
of the primary necessities of spiritual life. So understood, *Dubliners*
will be seen for what it is, in effect, both a group of short stories and
a novel, the separate histories of its protagonists composing one essential history, that of the soul of a people which has confused and weakened its relation to the source of spiritual life and cannot restore it.

In so far as this unifying action is evident in the realistic elements
of the book, it appears in the struggle of certain characters to escape
the constricting circumstances of existence in Ireland, and especially
in Dublin, "the centre of paralysis." As in *A Portrait of the Artist as
a Young Man,* an escape is envisaged in traveling eastward from the
city, across the seas to the freedom of the open world. In *Dubliners,*
none of Joyce's protagonists moves very far on this course, though
some aspire to go far. Often their motives are unworthy, their minds
are confused. Yet their dreams of escape and the longing of one of

them even to "fly away to another country" are suggestive of the intent
of Stephen Dedalus in *A Portrait* to "fly by those nets," those constrictions of "nationality, language, religion," which are fully represented
in *Dubliners* also. Thus, in both books, ideas of enclosure, of arrest,
and of movement in space are associated with action of moral purport
and with spiritual aspiration and development.

In *Dubliners,* the meaning of movement is further complicated by
the thematic import of that symbolic paralysis which Joyce himself
referred to, an arrest imposed from within, not by the "nets" of external circumstance, but by a deficiency of impulse and power. The
idea of a moral paralysis is expressed sometimes directly in terms of
physical arrest, even in the actual paralysis of the priest Father Flynn,
whose condition is emphasized by its appearance at the beginning
of the book and is reflected in the behavior of Father Purdon, in the
penultimate story "observed to be struggling up into the pulpit" as if
he were partially paralyzed. But sheer physical inaction of any kind
is a somewhat crude means of indicating moral paralysis. Joyce has
used it sparingly. The frustrations and degradations of his moral
paralytics are rarely defined in physical stasis alone, and are sometimes concomitant with vigorous action. Their paralysis is more often
expressed in a weakening of their impulse and ability to move force-
fully, effectually, far, or in the right direction, especially by their frustration in ranging eastward in the direction of release or by their
complete lack of orientation, by their failure to pass more than a little
way beyond the outskirts of Dublin, or by the restriction of their
movement altogether to the city or to some narrow area within it.

The case of the boy in the first story, "The Sisters," is representative. Restive under the surviving influence of his dead mentor Father
Flynn, yet lost without him, and resentful of the meager life of the
city, he only dreams vaguely and disturbingly of being in a far country
in the East, and wakes to wander in the city that still encloses him.
At the end of the story he sits among hapless women, all immobile and
disconsolate, in the dead priest's own room, in the very house where
the priest has died, near the center of the center of paralysis. His
physical arrest and his enclosure are expressive, even apart from a
knowledge of the rich symbolism which qualifies them in ways too
complicated to consider at this stage in discussion. Bereft of spiritual
guidance, and deprived of the tension of an interest that has been
primary in his life, he sits confused and in isolation, unsustained by
the secular world about him, unstirred by anything in the natural
world, moved only by a fleeting sense of life still in the coffin in the
room overhead, a doubt and a hope like a faint resurgence of faith,
instantly dispelled.

It should be no surprise to discover in a book developing the theme of moral paralysis a fundamental structure of movements and stases, a system of significant motions, countermotions, and arrests, involving every story, making one consecutive narrative of the surge and subsidence of life in Dublin. In the development of the tendency to eastward movement among the characters of *Dubliners,* and in its successive modifications, throughout the book, something of such a system is manifest. It may be characterized briefly as an eastward trend, at first vague, quickly becoming dominant, then wavering, weakening, and at last reversed. Traced in rough outline, the pattern is as follows: in a sequence of six stories, an impulse and movement eastward to the outskirts of the city or beyond; in a single story, an impulse to fly away upward out of a confining situation near the center of Dublin; in a sequence of four stories, a gradual replacement of the impulse eastward by an impulse and movement westward; in three stories, a limited activity confined almost wholly within the central area of Dublin; and in the concluding story a movement eastward to the heart of the city, the exact center of arrest, then, in vision only, far westward into death.

Interpreted realistically, without recourse to symbol, this pattern may show at most the frustration of Dubliners unable to escape eastward, out of the seaport and overseas, to a more living world. An orientation so loosely conceived seems quite unsuited to determine a powerful organization of form and meaning. Understood in its symbolic import, however, the eastward motion or the desire for it takes on a much more complicated and precise significance.

Orientation and easting are rich in symbolic meanings of which Joyce was certainly aware. An erudite Catholic, he must have known of the ancient though not invariable custom of building churches with their heads to the east and placing the high altar against the east wall or eastward against a reredos in the depths of the building, so that the celebrant of the mass faced east, and the people entered the church and approached the altar from the west and remained looking in the same direction as the priest. He knew that in doing so they looked toward Eden, the earthly paradise, and he may have felt, like Gregory of Nyssa, that the force of the sacramental orientation was increased by that fact. Perhaps he did not know that the catechumens of the fourth century turned to the west to renounce Satan and to the east to recite the creed before they stepped into the baptismal font, to receive the sacrament that opens the door of spiritual life. Probably he did know that Christ returning for the Last Judgment was expected to come from the east. And he must have shared that profound human feeling, older than Christianity, which has made the sunrise immemorially and all but universally an emblem of the return of life and has made the east, therefore, an emblem of beginning and a place of rebirth. Many times Joyce must have seen the sun rise out of the Irish Sea, washed and brilliant. He could not have failed to know that washing and regeneration are implicit in the sacrament of baptism, and he may have known that in the earlier ages of Christianity baptism was called Illumination. He could not have failed, and the evidence of his symbolism in *Dubliners* shows that he did not fail, to see how a multitude of intimations of spiritual meaning affected the eastward aspirations and movements of characters in his book, and what opportunity it afforded of giving to the mere motion of his characters the symbolic import of moral action.

In constructing *Dubliners,* Joyce must have responded to the force of something like the whole body of insights of which these are representative. For these insights, with some others closely associated with them, are the chief light by which we shall be enabled to follow the development of what I have called the unifying action of *Dubliners* and, through understanding the structure of the book, to penetrate to its central significance. The unity of *Dubliners* is realized, finally, in terms of religious images and ideas, most of them distinctively Christian.

Among these the most important for the immediate purpose of understanding are the symbols, sacraments, and doctrines of the Catholic Church, especially its version of the ancient sacraments of baptism and the sacrificial meal and its concepts of the soul's powers, its perils, and its destiny. In terms of the religious ideas with which Joyce was most familiar the basic characteristics of his structural scheme are readily definable, and some of them are not definable otherwise. The unifying action may be conceived of, oversimply yet with essential accuracy, as a movement of the human soul, in desire of life, through various conditions of Christian virtue and stages of deadly sin, toward or away from the font and the altar and all the gifts of the two chief sacraments provided for its salvation, toward or away from God. In these ideas all the most essential determinants of the spiritual action which makes of *Dubliners* one consecutive narrative are represented: its motivation, its goal and the means of reaching it, and those empowering or disempowering states of inmost being which define the moral conditions under which the action takes place.

The states of being, of virtue and sin, are doubly important. For in *Dubliners* the primary virtues and sins of Christian tradition function both in their intrinsic character, as moral manifestations and determinants of behavior, and structurally in defining the order of the separate stories and in integrating them in a significant sequence. Thus they are one means of establishing the unity of the book, a simple but not arbitrary or wholly superficial means, supplementing with structural reinforcement and with a deepening of import that more fundamental pattern of motions and arrests already touched upon.

Like the booklong sequence of movements and stases, the various states of the soul in virtue and sin form a pattern of strict design traceable through every story. Each story in *Dubliners* is an action defining amid different circumstances of degradation and difficulty in the environment a frustration or defeat of the soul in a different state of strength or debility. Each state is related to the preceding by conventional associations or by causal connections or by both, and the entire sequence represents the whole course of moral deterioration ending in the death of the soul. Joyce's sense of the incompatibility of salvation with life in Dublin is expressed in a systematic display, one by one in these stories, of the three theological virtues and the four cardinal virtues in suppression, of the seven deadly sins triumphant, and of the deathly consequence, the spiritual death of all the Irish. Far more than his announced intention, of dealing with childhood, adolescence, maturity, and public life, this course of degenerative change in the states of the soul tends to determine the arrangement of the stories in a fixed order and, together with the pattern of motions and arrests, to account for his insistence upon a specific, inalterable sequence.

Although Joyce's schematic arrangement of virtues and sins in *Dubliners* does not conform entirely to the most usual order in listing them, it does so in the main. In the first three stories, in which the protagonists are presumably innocent, the theological virtues faith, hope, and love, in the conventional order, are successively displayed in abeyance and finally in defeat. In the fourth story, the main character, Eveline, lacking the strength of faith, hope, and love, wavers in an effort to find a new life and, failing in the cardinal virtue of fortitude, remains in Dublin, short of her goal and weakened in her spiritual powers and defenses against evil. In the fifth through the eleventh stories the seven deadly sins, pride, covetousness, lust, envy, anger, gluttony, and sloth, are portrayed successively in action usually in association with other sins adjacent in the list. The seven stories devoted to the sins occupy exactly the central position in the book. The sequence of their presentation is the most conventional one, except for the placing of anger before gluttony, a slight and not unique deviation. Gluttony is strongly represented, moreover, in the usual position, the fifth place, by means of the drunkenness of the central character Farrington, as well as in the sixth. And in the sixth place gluttony is defined in the attitudes and behavior of others than the main character, Maria, who is interested in food and much concerned with it rather than avid of it. Her quiet depression is more truly expressive of her essential state of soul; and in it another sin that appears rarely in lists of the seven is apparent, the sin of tristitia, or gloominess, sometimes substituted for the similar sin of sloth. Joyce's intent seems to have been to create here a palimpsest, inscribing three sins in the space afforded for two. The effect has been to reduce gluttony to secondary importance while giving it full recognition in both of its aspects as overindulgence in drinking as well as in eating. The sequence of sins completes Joyce's representation of the defeat of the soul in its most inward strength and prepares for its failure in the exercise of rational powers. Alienated wholly from God, it cannot act now even in expression of the natural or cardinal virtues, in the words of Aquinas "the good as defined by reason." In the twelfth through the fourteenth stories, the subversion of the cardinal virtues of justice, temperance, and prudence, and the contradiction of reason, upon which they are based, is displayed in those narratives that Joyce intended to represent "public life" in Ireland. Justice, the social virtue regulating the others, comes first in the group. The placing of prudence or wisdom last instead of first, the commonest position, is perhaps influenced by the sequence of appearance in these stories of those hindrances of the spirit in Ireland the "nets" of "nationality, language, religion." The order, moreover, is climactic. Certainly the culminating subversion of the three virtues is represented in the third story of this group, "Grace," in the sermon of "a man of the world" recommending worldly wisdom for the guidance of "his fellowmen." In the fifteenth and last story of *Dubliners*, no virtue or sin is given such attention as to suggest its predominance. Perhaps that virtue of magnanimity which Aristotle added to the group of four named by the Greeks is displayed in abeyance in Gabriel Conroy's self-concern, but recovered at last in his final self-abnegation and visionary acceptance of the communion of death. Perhaps merely the consequences of moral degeneration are to be discerned in the final story, the completion of spiritual disintegration, death itself.

The pattern of virtues and sins and the spatial pattern of motions and arrests in *Dubliners* are of course concomitant, and they express one development. As sin flourishes and virtue withers, the force of the soul diminishes, and it becomes more and more disoriented, until at the last all the force of its impulse toward the vital east is confused and spent and it inclines wholly to the deathly west. All this development is embodied, realistically or symbolically, in the experience of the principal characters as they search for vital satisfaction either in spiritual wholeness or in personal willfulness, apprehending the nature of their goal and their immediate needs truly or falsely, moving effectually toward the means of spiritual enlargement or faltering into meanness and withdrawing into a meager and spurious safety, seeking or avoiding the sacred elements of the font and the altar, those

ancient Christian and pre-Christian means of sustaining the life of
the spirit through lustration, regeneration, illumination, and communion. The unifying pattern of motions and arrests is manifested,
story by story, in the action of the principal figure in each, as he moves
in relation to the orient source and to the sacramental resources of
spiritual life, expressing in physical behavior his moral condition of
virtue or sin and his spiritual need and desire. His activity, outwardly
of the body, is inwardly that of the soul, either advancing more or
less freely and directly eastward or else confined and halted or wandering disoriented, short of its true goal and its true objects the water
of regeneration and the wine and bread of communion, the means of
approach to God, and often in revulsion from them, accepting plausible substitutes or nothing whatever.

In *Dubliners* from first to last the substitutes are prominent, the
true objects are unavailable. The priest in the first story, "The Sisters,"
has broken a chalice, is paralyzed, and dies; he cannot offer communion, and an empty chalice lies on his breast in death. The food
and drink obtained by the boy whose friend he has been are unconse-
crated: wine and crackers are offered to him solemnly, but by secular
agents. Again and again throughout *Dubliners* such substitutes for the
sacred elements of the altar recur, always in secular guise: "musty
biscuits" and "raspberry lemonade," porter and "a caraway seed."
Suggestions less overt are no less pointed. The abundant table in "The
Dead," loaded with food and with bottled water and liquors, but
surrounded by human beings gathered together in imperfect fellow-
ship, emphasizes the hunger of the soul for bread and wine that can
nourish it, rather than the body, and assuage its loneliness through
restoring it to the communion of love. The symbolism of baptismal
water likewise enforces the fact of spiritual privation. In "The Sisters"
the secular baptism of a cold bath is recommended by the boy's uncle
as the source of his strength. Less certainly symbolic, but suggestive
in the context, is the fact that the body of the priest is washed by a
woman, a point that Joyce thought important enough to define by
explicit statements in two passages. In the house where the priest has
lived and died, his sisters keep a shop where umbrellas, devices for
rejecting the rain of heaven, are sold and re-covered. The open sea,
the great symbol of the font in *Dubliners,* is approached by many of
the central characters, longed for, but never embarked upon, never
really reached. Canal, river, and estuary are crossed; Kingstown
Harbor is attained, but the vessel boarded in the harbor is lying at
anchor. When, in fear of drowning, the reluctant protagonist of the
fourth story, "Eveline," hangs back refusing to embark on an ocean
voyage, she may be understood to have withdrawn as at the brink of
the baptismal font, for by her action she has renounced that new life

which she had looked forward to attaining through moving eastward out of Dublin Bay on the night sea. The idea of her deprivation is reinforced by her final condition, of insensate terror, the reverse of spiritual refreshment and illumination.

Though the spiritual objects that are imaged in these substitutes represent the gifts of the two chief sacraments of the Church, baptism, the first in necessity, and the Eucharist, the first in dignity, there is no suggestion in *Dubliners* that the soul's needs can be supplied by the Church, in its current condition. The only scene in a church, in the story "Grace," implies exactly the opposite, for the sermon of Father Purdon is frankly designed to serve the purposes of those who "live in the world, and, to a certain extent, for the world." The Church is secularized, and it shares in the general paralysis. Its failure in the lives of Joyce's Dubliners is emphasized by the irony that although the nature of the soul has not altered and the means of its salvation retain their old aspect, its needs must be satisfied in entire dissociation from the Church.

Since those needs cannot be satisfied in Ireland, as Joyce represents it in *Dubliners,* the soul's true satisfaction cannot be exhibited in the experience of those who remain in Ireland. It can only be simulated and suggested, either in their relation to those secular substitutes for spiritual things that intimate the need for baptism and communion or in their turning toward the soul's orient, the symbolic east, variously imaged. Some of Joyce's dissatisfied characters, such as Little Chandler, suppose that they can change their condition by escaping from Ireland eastward across the sea to another life in a different place. Physically their goal must be another country; spiritually it has the aspect of a new life. The association functions symbolically. Throughout *Dubliners,* one of the symbolic images of the spiritual goal is a far country. Like the symbols of water, wine, and bread, the far country images the soul's need for life that cannot be attained in Ireland.

Apparently it is not easily attainable outside of Ireland either. Those Dubliners who have reached England or the Continent, characters such as Gabriel Conroy or Ignatius Gallaher, the journalist whom Little Chandler envies because he has made a life for himself in London, show by their continuing to behave like other Dubliners that to be transported physically overseas is not necessarily to find a new life, or to be changed essentially at all. No doubt their failure to change means that the whole of Europe is secularized, perhaps the whole world. Still more, it emphasizes the subjective nature of the attainment symbolized by arrival in a far country. A new condition of inward life is the goal; not a place, but what the place implies, is the true east of the soul. The far countries reached by the boy in

"The Sisters" and sought by the boy in "Araby," perhaps the same
boy, are not in the world. In one story he dreams of being in an
eastern land which he thinks, not very confidently, is Persia. In
the other he goes to a bazaar bearing the "magical name" *Araby*, a
word casting "an Eastern enchantment." In both stories the far country is probably the same, that fabulous Arabia which is associated
with the Phoenix, symbol of the renewal of life in the resurrection
of the sun. To the dreamer it suggests a journey and strange customs,
but he cannot conceive its meaning. The meaning is plain, however,
to the reader aware of the symbols: the boy has looked inward toward
the source of his own life, away from that civilization which surrounds
him but does not sustain him. The same import, with further meaning, is apparent in the later story. The response of the boy to the name
Araby and his journey eastward across the city define his spiritual
orientation, as his response to the disappointing reality of the bazaar
indicates his rejection of a substitute for the true object of the soul's
desire.

The sea too, like the image and idea of a far country, symbolizes
the orient goal of life. It may of itself, as water, suggest the baptismal
font. And in any case it must tend strongly to do so because of the
sacramental import of water established by other water symbolism
throughout *Dubliners*. The element itself is highly significant, and
the great image of it is the sea, the water of liberating voyage and
of change and danger, of death and resurrection. The sheer physical
prominence of the sea eastward from Dublin colors the east with the
significance of baptismal water. In turn the sea is colored by the significance of the east. The altar, even more immediately than the font,
is implied in the concept of orientation.

Perhaps in the symbol of the sea in *Dubliners* the identification of
the two chief sacraments should be understood. Their identification
would not be altogether arbitrary. For the close relationship and even
the essential similarity of the two sacraments is suggested in several
ways, apart from their association with the east: by their interde-
pendence in fulfillment of a spiritual purpose; by the invariable mix-
ture of a few drops of water with the wine in the chalice; and above
all by the concept of rebirth, in which the font is profoundly associated
with the altar, the place where Christ is believed to be reborn at the
consecration of the divine sacrifice. That Joyce could make the identification is plain from his having merged font with altar in *Finnegans
Wake*, in the conception of the "tubbathaltar" of Saint Kevin Hydro-
philos. Going "westfrom" toward a suitable supply of water, and
showing his sense of the importance of orientation by genuflecting
seven times eastward, Saint Kevin fills up his device of dual function,
in "ambrosian eucharistic joy of heart," and sits in it. Though Joyce

may not have been ready, so early as in *Dubliners,* to identify font with altar, he has developed a body of symbolism which intimately involves them, and possibly merges them, in the symbol of the orient sea.

In that spatial pattern in which the unity of *Dubliners* is expressed as an action, the orient goal is no one simple thing. It is a rich complex of associated ideas and images, only outwardly a place or places, intrinsically a vital state of being, a condition of grace conferred and sustained, presumably, by all the means of grace. Perhaps the main aspect of the symbolic orient, however, is of the eastward sea, its richest and most constantly represented image. The sea is the image most clearly opposable to that deadly contrary of the symbolic orient in all its import of spiritual life, that deathly state of moral disability, which Joyce conceived to be dominant in Ireland and centered in Dublin. The opposition is basic and clear in *Dubliners* of the eastward sea to the westward land, of ocean water to earth, of movement to fixation, of vital change to passivity in the status quo, of the motion toward new life to the stasis of paralysis in old life ways.

Lesser symbols in *Dubliners* are understandable largely in terms of this opposition, the symbols of water, of color, of music, of clothing, and the various symbols of enclosure. Not even the predominant element of the sea, water itself, always implies the sea or its vital freedom. No doubt in its basic symbolic meaning water is conceivable truly enough in conventional terms as the water of life. But in *Dubliners* it is distinctly this only in a general sense, as it is also the natural water of the globe of earth and sky. For full understanding it must be viewed more exactly in terms of specific symbolism and associations. In the eastern sea, it is the water of the font and the chalice, toward which the soul is oriented. Sluggish in a canal beside which a wastrel walks with his tart, or as the ooze on the lavatory floor where a drunkard lies, at the opening of the story "Grace," it loses virtue. At the end of "Eveline," as the water of voyage which can carry the frightened girl from Ireland to a new life and to fulfilling love, it retains its basic meaning and values as well as those given it by its place in the symbolic complex of the sea.

The colors associated with the sea are established very emphatically in "An Encounter" by the boy narrator's finding to his surprise that none of the foreign sailors has the green eyes that he expected; their eyes are only blue, grey, or "even black." Truly green eyes, "bottle-green," appear to him only when he encounters the demonic gaze of the pervert on the bank in Ringsend near the Dodder. Thus green is dissociated from the sea and associated with degeneracy in Ireland, with crippling spiritual limitations, and with the physical limitation of enclosure in a bottle, an image suggesting water, but not the water of the open sea. The symbols of the bottle and of green are effectively

combined later in the book in the symbolic complex of the bottled
water on the table in "The Dead," pure water appropriately "white,"
but precisely marked with "transverse green sashes," the cancelling
strokes that declare the contents to be spiritually without virtue.
Among the ten colors mentioned in description of the table, and the
many more only suggested by the foods and drinks and the dishes
and bottles that are described, blue and grey do not appear, black is
mentioned once, and brown is markedly predominant. Brown, like
green, is associated with the limitations of life in Ireland, but much
more emphatically. It recurs many times in the stories. It is mentioned as the tint of Dublin streets and is found in the freckled face
and in the eyes of Miss Ivors, in "The Dead," who wears a brooch
with "an Irish device and motto" and is militantly Irish. Yellow and
red, the colors of fire, are variable in meaning, being associable at
one extreme with the vital orient, at another with the punishments of
the pit, as at the end of "A Painful Case."

The symbol of music is more clearly related to the east than to
the land, but it takes its meaning very largely from the context of
association and symbol in which it is represented. In "Eveline," where
it is associated with far countries and the sea, an Italian air played on
a street organ, the singing of a sailor about a sailor, and the quayside
whistle and bell of departure on an ocean voyage, music symbolizes
the motion of the soul toward life or the call of life to the soul. As
the remembered singing of Michael Furey in "The Dead," it is the
call to the past life, to communion with the dead.

Since clothing is an expression of character or of personal preference, or an indication of occupation or other circumstance, its symbolic use is restricted by the requirements of naturalism, the need to
conform to objective fact. Its symbolic meaning is given unequivocally
only in images associated with it at the free will of the artist. The
blackness of Father Flynn's clothing is less certainly symbolic than
its green discoloration, but the "suit of greenish-black" worn by the
pervert in "An Encounter" is indubitably symbolic in both its hues,
since Joyce was free in his choice of both. The "brown-clad" girl
worshipped by the boy in "Araby" is a madonna emphatically Irish.
Lenehan, in "Two Gallants," is clothed in unmistakable contradic-
tions. His "light waterproof" and "white rubber shoes" express an
aversion to water, as W. Y. Tindall has pointed out. It must be noted,
however, that he is also wearing a yachting cap, a suggestion of inclination toward the water of the sea. His waterproof, moreover, is
"slung over one shoulder in toreador fashion," suggesting the far
country of Spain, another symbol of the soul's orient. The symbolism
precisely defines his position as a vagrant, a drifter in the city, neither
committed to the ways of life in Dublin nor free of them. Generally

regarded as a "leech," he seems to be a creature of the pools and
streams of the earth, not of the sea. He belongs to the dregs of the
established world.

Certain images in *Dubliners,* of closed or circumscribed areas, such
as coffin, confession-box, rooms, buildings, the city and its suburbs,
become symbolic when they are presented in any way suggesting
enclosure, as they frequently are; and by recurrence many of them
are early established as conventional symbols. In general they express
the restrictions and fixations of life in Ireland. Except for the city
itself and its suburbs, the commonest of these symbolic images are the
houses of the people of Dublin, which are so well characterized in
Stephen Hero as "those brown brick houses which seem the very
incarnation of Irish paralysis." Such is the home, no doubt, of Little
Chandler in the story "A Little Cloud," who supposes himself to be
a prisoner simply in the external circumstances of his existence, though
really he is afflicted with the prevailing paralysis, the psychic limitation of his commitment to the ways of a society without vitality. Like
Eveline of the story that bears her name, who leaves for a while the
"little brown houses of her neighborhood," in one of which she lives,
Chandler cannot escape the constriction which those houses symbolize.
Surely his house too must be of symbolically brown brick, situated
somewhere near those houses referred to in *Stephen Hero,* which are
in Eccles Street, in the north central part of Dublin, at the very center
of paralysis.

Both the purpose and the length of this paper preclude discussion
of all the symbolism of *Dubliners.* Enough of it has been defined in
the preceding exposition, however, to make possible a brief and suffi-
ciently clear account of the stories in sequence, as a means of displaying
the outlines of the unifying action of the book in its essential character.
To avoid reiteration, I will refrain from pointing out the import of
the symbolism at every turn. The reader will no doubt find it prefer-
able to bear in mind the meaning of the chief symbolic images and
their main function in the symbolic pattern and to be constantly active
in discernment. I will, however, make whatever interpretations may
be required by the purpose of the discussion, to reveal the single action
of *Dubliners* in the separate actions of the principal figures, story by
story to trace in their diverse histories the symbolically significant
motions and arrests and to discover in them the one composite movement of the agonistic soul of the Irish through stage after stage of its
decline.

In the first story of *Dubliners,* "The Sisters," the sterility of Irish
life is defined. As a naturalistic narrative, it is an account of a boy's
deprivation of spiritual guidance and support, through the death of

his friend the priest Father Flynn, a paralytic who has committed the ecclesiastical crime of simony, a sin implying worldliness, and has broken a chalice. His spiritual impotence even in life is made apparent by symbolic means. Sitting in a stupor, enclosed in his little dark room in his sisters' house that is also a shop, he spills through trembling fingers a powder of snuff. As odorous "clouds of smoke" it resembles incense, descending rather than rising. As "clouds" being "dribbled" in "showers," it has the aspect also of a liquid. Dropping from the hands that have broken a chalice, it is a dusty successor to the sacramental wine. Brown, like the earth of Ireland, it tinges his black garments with green.

When the priest is dead, his sisters Nannie and Eliza assume his place and functions in a significant scene. Nannie's name and the appearance of her shoes "trodden down all to one side" suggest a goat, or worse. In the strangeness of her feet and in the clumsy way "her skirt was hooked at the back" she resembles the celebrant of the black mass in the Circe episode of *Ulysses,* who has "two left feet back to the front" and wears "a long petticoat and reversed chasuble." When the boy and his aunt visit the home of the dead priest and she performs the hospitable actions paralleling imperfectly the ceremony of the Eucharist, her evil aspect is a means of emphasizing the invalid character of the sacramental action. Essentially, however, she is a feckless old woman who does wrong in ignorance. Eliza, just as innocently usurping the position of the dead priest, is "seated in his armchair in state." She tells Nannie to pour the wine, and when she sits silent the others wait respectfully for her to speak. Her position, given force by her authority, suggests that of a bishop or pope, whose chair or throne can symbolize his state.

The futility of the spurious ritual is emphasized by two references to the empty fireplace, dark since the death of the priest. The symbolic import of the image is confirmed and defined by a parallel in *A Portrait of the Artist as a Young Man*: the dean of studies, seen kindling a fire, "seemed . . . a humble server making ready the place of sacrifice in an empty temple." The boy, moreover, refuses the ministration of the women. He rejects the crackers, the bread, the one element administered to the laity in communion, and takes up the wine from the table himself, the element reserved for the priest, as if he were sensible of the "great wish" that the priest has had for him, or as if he were conscious of the implications of his recent dream in which the priest has attempted to confess to him as to a priest. The suggestions in this dream of the assumption of spiritual responsibility by the boy and of his journeying to a churchlike place in the East, where there are "long curtains and a swinging lamp of antique fashion," define the need of Dubliners to seek out for themselves the spiritual life that is no longer available in Ireland.

In this story, however, the need for reorientation of the soul is no further defined than in these intimations. At the end, the boy and his companions are reminded of the priest in life, "in the dark of his confession-box" alone and laughing in his mild dementia, and they listen briefly for some similar token of life remaining in the coffin. Hearing no sound, the boy understands with apparent finality that the paralysis of Father Flynn is complete in death. Perhaps the death of God is intimated, for the priest lies overhead, and, moreover, in a stroke of wit Joyce has given him in the very first sentence of the book an aspect of God, in stating that hope for his life was abandoned at the third onset of his malady, as if his death must be threefold. The surmise is made more plausible by the fact that, like that "half-witted God of the Roman Catholics" scorned by the Stephen of *Stephen Hero,* the priest has not been for some time wholly himself. Whatever we may wish to make of this, the fact remains that the boy, an orphan, is bereaved of his fatherly friend and is left without other spiritual authority to guide him than his own powers. Though these have been vaguely suggested in his dream he has no reason to have faith in them.

In the first story of *Dubliners* the action takes place in or near the priest's home in Great Britain Street, near the center of Dublin, and though the boy dreams of a far country he does not conceive of going there or understand that he can move beyond the limits of his circumstances. The symbolic orient does not draw him. This is a story of the soul suspended in almost complete arrest, only vaguely sensing its orient and its powers.

In the second story, "An Encounter," a boy who lives in the northeast part of the city moves southeastward, across the Liffey, to wander in Ringsend. The expedition is a disorderly adventure of truants from a Catholic school, who "break out of the weariness of school-life for one day." Inspired by stories of the Wild West, they have spent their evenings in disorderly play that has seemed liberating but at last has become wearisome. The narrator begins to desire real adventures, but he understands that "they must be sought abroad." With another boy he plans to go along the Wharf Road until they reach the shipping by the quays, to cross in the ferry, and to visit the Pigeon House, a fort at the mouth of the Liffey, a mile east of Ringsend. The name of their eastward goal is symbolic, since the pigeon, or rock dove, is an emblem of the Holy Ghost. Accomplishing all but the last part of their plan, they admire a Norwegian vessel, observe the sea-colored eyes of the sailors, and remain in Ringsend to eat musty biscuits and

chocolate and to drink pink lemonade and to idle away their after-
noon. Their hope of escape does not carry them so far eastward as
they desire, but it brings them into contact with a pervert, green-eyed
and dressed in "greenish-black," the hellish image of that spirit of
disorder which has moved them. The implication is that in Ireland
the choice for those who would have "real adventures" lies between
degradation and conventional order. In this story, though the un-
satisfied soul moves a little way eastward, in the hope of escape into
life, it is quickly frustrated.

In "Araby," the third story, as in the first, the absence of spiritual
sustenance in Dublin is symbolized by the death of a priest. The
enclosure of musty air in the house where he has died is suggestive of
staleness in the very breath of life which he has ceased to animate,
and the fact that he has been a "very charitable priest" is a reminder
of that Christian virtue of love which in this story is portrayed as
flourishing briefly before its dispersal. Outside, however, the evening
sky has the liturgical color of violet and the air has a vital sting, the
lamps of Dublin glow, there is music of shaken harness, and Mangan's
sister stands on the doorstep. Her dress swings, the "rope of her hair"
is "tossed." In this imagery there is vital motion and a slight suggestion of the sea, symbol of the soul's orient. If the Church lacks spiritual life, the natural life of man may be elevated to take its place.
By his idealizing love, the boy narrator may restore the spiritual life
of the secular city, worshipping his madonna in eucharistic rituals as
if he would assume the powers of priest in a new faith. Leaving his
home in the northeast part of Dublin, he journeys in an empty train
across the water of the Liffey to a far place of eastern appearance and
name, the bazaar *Araby*, where he hopes to obtain a gift for her, some
confirmation of the life that exalts him. Hope, faith, and love itself
are destroyed when, at his goal, he finds the bazaar about to close,
silent like "a church after a service," and at its center the vulgar at-
tendants conversing and counting money. The soul's energy has carried it across water but not to the sea, far eastward but to a secular
goal, not to its true orient.

The central figure in the story "Eveline" lives in the state of deprivation determined by the failure of faith, hope, and love in the triad
of earlier stories. She is the first of the characters in *Dubliners* to
attempt, in the course of any story, to escape from Ireland and cross
the water to a far country and new life; and she is the last. Her
situation is unique: innocent of sin, yet old enough for independence,
she is morally free enough to escape. But she lacks the necessary
moral force. Offered a life in Buenos Ayres by a young man, a former
sailor, who loves her, she consents to leave her home and her drunken,
abusive father. But at the North Wall, due eastward from the center

of Dublin, the black ship appalls her, and she clutches the iron railing in frenzied fear of drowning. Her fiercely energetic action is symbolic of her moral paralysis, an inability to move to the baptism of the night journey over water and the communion of love in a new life. And at the same time it is actual arrest. At the end, Eveline is "passive, like a helpless animal," as if soulless, paralyzed by fear. Lacking the virtue of fortitude that strengthens the soul for compliance with the dictates of reason, she must turn back from danger and from life. Her plight exemplifies the state of the soul enclosed in the barren homeland because it is too weak to cross the threshold of the east.

With "After the Race," the concourse of sins commences, inevitably with the sin of pride. The suppression of the soul that in "Eveline" caused its withdrawal from action and reduced the girl to the semblance of an animal, is seen in this fifth story to have opened the way for an extraordinary ebullience of material energy. The sweep of movement is greater than in any other story: it begins far to the west of Dublin and ends in Kingstown Harbor. Thus pride comes out of the west, the direction contrary to the vital east. Both physical and financial power are depicted in exaltation, most compellingly in the central symbol of the opening scenes, a costly motor car, "a swift blue animal," which by exacting response from "the machinery of human nerves" reverses the roles of man and mechanism. The hero of the story, Jimmy Doyle, is a grey-eyed young man with a brown mustache, colors identified with the symbolic opposites of sea and land and defining precisely his spiritual condition, between the poles of good and evil. In him the state of the soul that has lost its virtue and stands at the threshold of sin is represented. His disposition toward pride is indicated early by his pleasure in the notoriety brought by his riding with wealthy foreigners in the car, and later by his feeling "the lack of an audience" when he finds himself in glittering circumstances aboard a yacht. His parents feel "a certain pride" because of his associations with the men and names of foreign cities. His triumph is accompanied by the sound of music: motor horns, gongs of trams, singing, and the piano music of a penniless Hungarian. It culminates in a night of card-playing and drunkenness aboard a yacht that rests nightlong on the symbolic waters of a harbor. The stationary voyage ends in stasis and stupor. Jimmy, like Eveline, resembles in the end a paralyzed animal.

The degradation of the soul continues in "Two Gallants," with a disreputable sexual adventure in which money is the primary object. As Levin and Shattuck have pointed out in their essay, the "fine decent tart" whom Lenehan covets and Corley enjoys is a debased Nausicaa, princess of a seagoing people and befriender of Odysseus. The tart wears clothing suggestive of the sea, a blue serge skirt, white blouse and sailor hat, and a black jacket with mother-of-pearl buttons; and her eyes are blue. The impression is complicated by other details: at her bosom are red flowers, stems up, inverted perhaps to symbolize her barren nature, and her slack mouth with projecting teeth lies open, monstrously. She is not wholly a succoring princess, though Corley relies on her for goldpieces; she is no angel of the waters, but a gutter sprite. Corley's first encounter with her, begun "under Waterhouse's clock," included a walk beside a canal and an excursion into a field in Donnybrook, through which flows the Dodder, of ugly associations in "An Encounter." Accompanied by Lenehan, Corley goes from Rutland Square, at the top of O'Connell Street, through the center of Dublin and southeast to Hume Street to meet her, then, leaving Lenehan, east with her to Merrion Square, where they board the Donnybrook tram that carries them southeast. Lenehan retraces his path across Dublin, turns west at Rutland Square, and circles back to his rendezvous with Corley. On the way he stops for a solitary meal of peas and ginger beer, and to meditate the possibility of marrying for money. He meets Corley, who displays in his hand what he has obtained from the tart, the gold coin, final object of his symbolic communion, the body and blood of the sacrifice counterfeited in gold. For both men the essential value in life is money, and their sin is avarice. The soul's primary movement in this story is southeastward to the debased substitute for communion and the symbolic waters, then westward in a partial return. Secondarily, as the movement of Lenehan, it is a circular motion about the center of the city.

The circular motion of Lenehan prefigures the confinement of movement in the next story, "The Boarding House," in which all the action takes place in the house, in Hardwick Street, just north of Rutland Square. There the soul is arrested, virtually at the center of Dublin. In "The Boarding House" the main concern of the minor characters is money, for which a mother sacrifices her honor and her daughter's virtue, and for which the man they trick goes unwillingly into the bondage of marriage. The object of his lust, the sin which he has confessed to a priest, is "a little perverse madonna" whose eyes are "grey with a shade of green." Glimpsed in her role of temptress, she wears a "loose open combing jacket," and the virgin white of her instep appears against the animal fur of her slippers. The symbolic indications of her relation to the spiritual orient are exact: her virginal aspect is vulgarized and contradicted, and her eyes tinged with pool-green symbolize at most the sea's ambivalent margins. She is the foam-born goddess of earthly love, a debased Aphrodite, as Levin and Shattuck have shown her to be in the Homeric parallel also. Her temple is a boarding house which is beginning to acquire "a certain fame" and which is managed by a woman referred to by the boarders

as "the Madam." Though her lover thinks of escape, he is constrained
by social pressures, by concern for his business position, and by uneasiness about his sin. Longing "to ascend through the roof and fly away
to another country," he descends to the parlor to agree to the marriage.
The suggestion of upward motion toward the spiritual orient is
countered by an actual downward movement toward the secular
substitute.

The limitation of movement in this story is an emphatic expression
of a new stage in the unifying action of the book. For the impulse to
move eastward beyond Dublin is reduced to a fantasy, and it is never
after this point restored, except in "A Painful Case," and then only to
be suppressed in revulsion. In "A Little Cloud," the eighth and central
story of *Dubliners,* the fantasy is continued in Little Chandler's brief
dream of literary success, which is engendered by his envy of his
friend Gallaher, who has become a journalist in London. Nursing a
vague hope of visiting London as a successful poet, Little Chandler
walks toward the fashionable bar where he is to meet Gallaher, going
east and southeast, down Capel Street and across Grattan Bridge over
the Liffey, the route that Lenehan followed in the second part of his
circular stroll while waiting for Corley. Like the sun god of myth,
Gallaher has blue eyes, though his are not perfectly blue, and his gold
watch and "vivid orange tie," twice mentioned, suggest the glow of
the god. Dazzled, and warmed by his heavily watered drink, Little
Chandler timorously enjoys his brief communion, at the same time
painfully considering the injustice of the contrast between himself
and his friend. At home, he regretfully contrasts the composure of
his prim wife's eyes with the Oriental eyes of Jewesses available to
Gallaher. When the crying of the baby breaks into his reading of
Byron, he rebels at his hopeless imprisonment in "his little house,"
and shouting at the child he frightens it into paroxysms. It is almost
beyond doubt that he has come home to this defeat across O'Connell
Bridge and past Rutland Square; for, as we have seen, the likeliest
location of his home is in the neighborhood of Eccles Street. He has
probably made a circuit coinciding almost perfectly with Lenehan's
movement about the center of the city.

A similar circling occurs in "Counterparts," the next story, when
after leaving the office in Eustace Street the central character, Farrington, goes eastward to make the round of the bars, from Davy Byrne's
south of O'Connell Bridge to Mulligan's somewhat east of it. The
circling expresses his true desire, for he has come in anger and revulsion from the office, where he has been humbled by his superior, Mr.
Alleyne, and he goes home, eastward to the suburb of Sandymount,
with the bitterest loathing. The vital image toward which he is impelled, but without hope of attainment, is a woman with a London

accent, wearing a peacock-blue scarf and gloves of bright yellow, the orient colors of sea and sun. But her eyes are brown, and he encounters her in Mulligan's in Poolbeg Street just east of the center of Dublin. Farrington's whole desire is concentrated upon central Dublin, where he hopes to restore his sensations of power and self-esteem, through drunkenness, sexual conquest, and a display of physical strength. But he is overcome in a show of strength, and his money runs out before he can accomplish his first two objects. In Sandymount he vents his anger and asserts his superiority by caning his little boy. His story shows the weakening of the disoriented soul as sin more and more alienates it from God.

In the next story, "Clay," the drift of the soul toward death begins. The central character, Maria, journeys away from the waters, symbolized by the *Dublin by Lamplight* laundry where she works. In this curious name, suggesting soiled water and artificial light, baptism both as washing and as illumination is implied. The barmbracks cut and served for tea by Maria are an intimation of the host, divided before the ritual and mechanically apportioned, exactly four pieces to each woman served. Both of the chief sacraments are represented in the symbolism of the false orient of the soul at which Maria's journey begins. The sacrament of marriage is represented by the ring mentioned by one of the laundresses, a Hallow Eve charm which Maria desires but never receives. Maria is a tiny, disappointed spinster with the grey-green eyes that combine the symbolic colors of sea and stagnant pools, appropriate for a laundress. Riding the tram from Ballsbridge to Drumcondra, she goes from the southeastern suburb, through the center of Dublin, to the northern suburb, stopping at the Pillar in O'Connell Street to buy gifts of food for her relatives. On the ride to Drumcondra, her spiritual inclinations are emphasized by her encounter with an ambiguous figure, a half-drunk elderly red-faced stout man with greyish mustache and brown hat. When he makes room for her to sit down she contrasts him with the young men, who have ignored her. The three topics of his conversation, Hallow Eve, the rain, and the food in her bag, are reminders of the three sacraments earlier represented. Maria's pleasure in him is misplaced, for she receives nothing from him. Instead, she suffers a loss. In her happy confusion, she forgets her package of plumcake. Or perhaps he actually steals it. The suspicion, coupled with his stoutness, his drunkenness, and his talk of the enjoyment of food, is enough to associate him with the sin of gluttony. Amid the heavy emphasis upon food and drink throughout the story, Maria appears almost abstemious. Her downcast shyness and wistful disappointment in her lonely life seem evidence that her soul's defect is gloominess, the sin of *tristitia*. The impression is strengthened by her turning somewhat westward, away from the orient. She is ready for death, as her touching the clay in the Hallow Eve games intimates.

James Duffy, hero of "A Painful Case," actually lives in the far western suburb of Chapelizod, though he is a banker in Baggot Street in southeast Dublin. He lives "without any communion with others," withdrawn even from himself, thinking of himself in the third person and the past tense, somewhat as if he were no longer in life. His sin is sloth. Yet he interrupts his deathly abstraction by an intellectual intimacy that carries him eastward to Dublin concert halls and to the southeastern seaside suburb of Sydney Parade into the home of a Mrs. Sinico, blue-eyed, the neglected wife of a sea captain. When at Duffy's insistence upon the soul's loneliness she makes a gesture of affection, he withdraws from her in fear and rectitude and so deprives them both of the communion of life. Years later, reading of her drunken death, perhaps suicide, he hastens in revulsion from Dublin to Chapelizod, but is drawn eastward again to the western edge of Dublin, the scene of his last parting with her in Phoenix Park. It is a movement toward life, in yearning for contact, but though the name of the park suggests a resurrection, he finds there only a final realization that he is "outcast from life's feast," from communion. Aware of his responsibility for Mrs. Sinico's death under the wheels of a train, he wanders in his lonely night, turning his eyes first to the sea-grey river "winding along towards Dublin," eastward; then to its contrary image, a far freight train "winding out of Kingsbridge Station, like a worm with a fiery head winding through the darkness, obstinately and laboriously," westward. He hears its rhythm repeating her name. His sense of guilt, the image as of a worm of death and hell, and the heartlike thud of its noise in his ears, combine in an impression of his identification with the destroyer. Turning homeward, he will go in the same direction as the train. It is a symbolic movement of the soul toward death, a suitable conclusion of the action in sin that began with a proud eastward plunge of mechanical energy.

Hereafter in *Dubliners* the disoriented, unregenerate, unnourished soul, alienated from God by sin, acts only at the center of paralysis and looks beyond it only toward death. The characters in the last four stories move no farther to the east than the central areas of the city, they depend on the meager resources of life in Dublin, and their aspiration toward vital satisfaction beyond the present time and scene is directed to a future that has the aspect of the dead past.

In the three stories of public life that follow "A Painful Case," the culminating action occurs in one building or another within three quarters of a mile of O'Connell Bridge, approximately the center of Dublin. In "Ivy Day in the Committee Room," the uneasy canvassers for the Nationalist candidate Tierney assemble to wait for their un-

certain payment at the headquarters in Wicklow Street just south of
the Bridge. Here the political life of the city and of the country as a
whole is focused with symbolic force. The aged caretaker who tends
the unwilling fire and sets out the bottles of brown stout has "moist
blue eyes" and a mechanically munching mouth, and the canvasser
O'Connor who sits with him has grey hair and a pimply face. Before
the other canvassers return, a man with a brown mustache and rain-
drops on his hat, Joe Hynes, not of their group, steps into the room
and twice asks, " 'What are you doing in the dark?' " Candles are
lighted, the physical darkness is diminished; Mr. Henchy enters, and
Hynes remains long enough to defend the right of the working-man
to run for office and to condemn both Tierney, whom no one trusts,
and the English King, whose visit to Ireland Mr. Henchy approves of
because it will bring "an influx of money." The ambiguous figure of
Father Keon appears, dubiously suggestive of priest and actor. His
"very bright blue eyes" and rainwet face like "yellow cheese" give him
the symbolic aspect of the orient god of the sun. Though the impression is modified by the quality of the yellow, it is strengthened by the
"rosy spots" on the cheeks and by the shining of his buttons in the
candlelight. His black clothing may symbolize the night sea, or the
divine darkness, or the darkness of evil and death. He is called a
"black sheep" and he goes to transact some business with a politician
at the *Black Eagle*. His refusal of light on the dark stairs, where he
"can see" to descend, suggests self-generated light, like that of the sun
or of God. These and other indications in him of obscured divinity
give him the aspect of a spiritual power in decline. Thus he is a symbolic apparition of a force supplanted by the present leader Tierney,
by King Edward VII, and at the end of the story by Parnell, whom
Hynes returns to praise in a poem as "Our Uncrowned King." Led by
Hynes, all look to the political force of a life that has vanished in the
past. Admired by all, Hynes' poem represents the hope of Ireland as
dependent upon the resurrection of the betrayed leader, compared to
Christ and the Phoenix, in a world manifestly as barren of justice
and as hostile to spiritual life as when he was "slain."

In the thirteenth story, "A Mother," the center of action lies somewhat farther to the east, in the Antient Concert Rooms on Great
Brunswick Street, less than half a mile southeast of O'Connell Bridge.
Mrs. Kearney, the main character, has lost all traces of an early superficial affinity for the east, symbolized by her "ivory manners" as a
girl and by her habit of "eating a great deal of Turkish delight." She
respects her brown-bearded husband for his solid fixity, which gives
her a sense of security. She turns the Irish Revival to her daughter's
advantage by having her taught Irish as a means of advancing her
popularity. She cultivates Nationalist friends and musical friends,

with the effect of establishing the girl's reputation in Dublin musical circles as a pianist with pleasing personality and the right outlook. When given an opportunity to manage her daughter's talent, she is energetic and able. But upon the esthetic and financial failure of a series of concerts for which her daughter has been engaged as an accompanist, she ruins the girl's career by an unreasonable, intemperate concern for money and a display of ill feeling, bad taste, and manners anything but ivory. The fecklessness of the management, the mediocrity of the performers, the indecorum of the audience, and the cupidity and uncurbed passion of Mrs. Kearney reveal the disabling deficiency both of force and of control among those concerned with the arts in Ireland. The esthetic life of Dubliners is symbolized by an apparition, the wraithlike figure of a soprano, Madam Glynn, imported from London to sing at the concerts. Her appearance as of one "resurrected from an old stage-wardrobe," the faded condition of her blue dress, and her "bodiless gasping voice" suggest the vanquished life of a former time. In the ghostly image the remoteness of the symbolic east and the feebleness of its influence are made apparent.

At the beginning of the fourteenth story, "Grace," which was for a time the final story of *Dubliners,* the principal character, Mr. Kernan, is seen at the end of a drunken bout, in degradation and immobility, "quite helpless," lying "curled up at the foot of the stairs down which he had fallen," on the filthy floor of a basement lavatory in a bar in south central Dublin. After his fall—not from grace, for that has occurred long before, but from the dead level of decency in Dublin— he lies as if paralyzed, or as if dead in the womb of earth awaiting a call to resurrection which he can hardly expect to profit by. The story ironically represents the futile efforts of Dubliners to elevate him. In the bar he is rescued by Mr. Power, a fair man in a yellow ulster, the color of orient light, but without a trace of symbolic blue about him, and taken across Dublin to his home on the Glasnevin Road, the northwest outskirts. Glimpsed in his seat on the car, as it nears O'Connell Bridge at the heart of the city, Mr. Kernan appears as if in his original attitude on the floor, though set upright, "huddled together with cold" before the biting east wind that blows upriver from the sea. In his bedroom, two days later, he is seen in much the same position, "propped up in bed," while his friends plot to "make a new man of him" by persuading him to join them in a retreat, to confess his sins, and renew his "baptismal vows." His wife has denied him any of the stout served to his friends, but when he consents to join the retreat a neighbor, fair-haired like Mr. Power, suddenly appears with a bottle of "special whiskey," and all join in a round of drinks. The group look to the past, praising "the old, original faith" and old-fashioned education, and final plans are made for the retreat. Mr. Kernan refuses, however, to hold a lighted candle in the ceremony, and in doing so he symbolically rejects illumination. In the final scene, in the Jesuit Church in Gardiner Street, three quarters of a mile north of O'Connell Bridge, the friends are led by a priest, whom they rightly characterize as "a man of the world like ourselves," to the happy discovery that the attainment of grace requires of them no thought or act in the least contradictory of their worldly wisdom or more regular worldly behavior. While the casuist in the pulpit attacks the foundations of the cardinal virtue of prudence, or wisdom, Mr. Kernan and his friends kneel in the symbolic attitude first defined in his position amid the filth and ooze of the lavatory floor. Earlier Mr. Kernan, a former Protestant, having erred in a reference to the body of a church, has called it the "pit," as if he were thinking of a theater. But his tongue has found the word for *hell*. Obviously appropriate for the lavatory, it characterizes a church like that in which these Dubliners are last seen, kneeling in the polysymbolic attitude of drunken paralysis, of shrinking from the breath of the soul's orient, of the sickbed, and of supplication that we know to be hopeless because it is directed to the god of this world, the "mammon of iniquity" named in Father Purdon's text.

After this story, anything further might seem superfluous. The paralyzed soul has come to a dead halt, the end of its divagations, before a lifeless altar at "the centre of paralysis." Joyce may have asked himself, however, what would happen if the dead should recognize and accept their death. Whatever else the final story of *Dubliners* may be, it is an answer to this question. Recognition and acceptance would bring liberation, though not into life, and movement, though not to the east and not of the body. This story, "The Dead," shows a new development in *Dubliners,* a mitigation of the punishment of the enclosed and paralyzed. The physical movement of the main character Gabriel Conroy from a house in the western part of the city eastward to a hotel at the very center expresses in spatial terms his commitment to the ways and the doom of his fellow Dubliners. His spiritual movement westward, in imaginative vision, symbolizes his transcendence of that doom through recognition of its meaning and acceptance of the truth of his inward nature.

But this is the conclusion of the action of a long story. When first seen, coming in from the night, his clothing dusted with that symbolic snow the deathly import of which has been noted often, Gabriel brings a "fragrant" breath of chill air. He seems to represent in a vivid image the "dead" of Dublin who are foregathering in a house on Usher's Island, nearly a mile west of O'Connell Bridge, the home of his aging spinster aunts and cousin, who are giving their annual party for their friends and their music pupils. Gabriel is dissatisfied and uneasy, and he longs for the pure snowy air on the quay. In part he is pressed by his responsibility as toastmaster with a speech to make in praise of the tawdry artificial little world of his cousin and his kindly, moribund aunts. In part he is pained by a sense of his own futility and falsity. Attacked playfully as a "West Briton" by brown-eyed, Irish-speaking Miss Ivors, because he is not enthusiastic about his country and plans a vacation in Europe rather than the Aran Islands, Gabriel answers, " 'I'm sick of my own country, sick of it!' " Like the characters in the earlier stories, he longs to escape out of Ireland. His difference is that his deep inclination is toward the west rather than toward the east. When he looks toward the snowy night or thinks of walking upriver from Usher's Island, in Phoenix Park and "the white field of Fifteen Acres" at its center, it is not only the night and snow that allure him but the west itself.

Galway and the Aran Islands are not far enough, however. They represent the goal of the one Dubliner, Miss Ivors, who will not be wholly identified with the group at the party. Though constricted by her insistent overemphasis upon Ireland, she is honest and warm. The symbolism of color discriminates her from those Dubliners who are not only constricted in their life but corrupted by it. Mr. Browne, tediously insisting that he is "all brown," is not really so: he wears a "green overcoat," the color associated with symbolically stagnant water, and its "mock astrakhan" trimmings further define his false orientation. It is Miss Ivors who is "all brown," all Irish. Her refusal of supper is a rejection, symbolically, of communion in the house of the dead. Leaving the party early, she walks home alone, up the quay, westward, going the way of Gabriel's desire, though not to his ultimate goal.

Gabriel remains to preside at his aunts' table and to praise the ladies of the household and their preservation of the old-fashioned Irish hospitality, and to discredit the present "less spacious age." Thus the past is opened before him as a pleasant prospect, sentimentalized, suggesting also, however, changes and "absent faces" of the dead, from which he feels it proper to turn again to "living duties and living affections," to the present scene that is dominated by the "Three Graces of the Dublin musical world." Gabriel's fulsome exaltation of this feeble trinity shows his insensitiveness to the life of the present.

The music of the past dominates the night, moreover. In conversation the guests have dwelt upon great singers of the past, Italian and English, performers hardly to be matched in the present day, except, as Bartell D'Arcy insists, in London, Paris, and Milan. And as the company disbands, toward dawn, the music of the past is sounded by D'Arcy's tenor voice, singing a song "in the old Irish tonality." For Gabriel and his wife Gretta it is arresting. He is "surprised at her stillness" as she stands listening. Shadow darkens the ruddy colors of her skirt to black and white, the earthly terra cotta, and the salmon pink that suggests, however obliquely, the sea and the return of life from the sea to the land. She is an ambiguous image. Colors of land and sea appear also in her bronze hair and blue hat. To Gabriel she suggests a picture, which he would entitle *"Distant Music."* It calls him both toward her and to their past, their youth together. While they ride toward the hotel where they will pass the remainder of the night, waves of joy break upon his memory like "fire of stars," and he imagines the "old rattling box" of the cab is carrying them eastward out of Ireland "to catch the boat, galloping to their honeymoon."

Just before leaving his aunts' house Gabriel has revealed exactly the nature of the escape he is launched upon. Walking round and round in the hall, he has mimicked the action of an old horse, trained to the treadmill, that when driven in the streets has perversely circled around a statue. Gabriel has just finished a speech in praise of the past, to which all monuments are built. In the cab, which he believes will carry him to a renewal of old delight, he is going forward only to a travesty of the dead past, found as if by traveling in a circle. Such movement, constricted by conventions of the soul, is really spiritual arrest, the psychic paralysis of the treadmill, in *Stephen Hero* aptly described as a "stationary march."

In their room, in the Gresham Hotel on the east side of O'Connell Street not far north of the Bridge, Gabriel dismisses the porter and sends the candle with him. Perhaps his wish is to be lighted only by the fire of his joy. But a "ghastly light" of the street lamp lays a long streak from the western window to the locked door; the blasting light of Dublin illumines the room. Turned there to the past, in hope of resurrecting his life by embracing his wife in the spirit of their early days of marriage, Gabriel does not understand that in having "escaped from their lives and duties" he has rejected the present and moved toward death. And he discovers too late that his wife has made a similar movement away from life, but not toward him. Stirred by D'Arcy's song to her own memories, Gretta like Gabriel has turned to the past and given herself to the image of love there. But what she remembers is a grave, that of the boy Michael Furey, who she believes died for her. Moving away from their present life, which has not sustained them spiritually, the living are not united, for their motion is toward diverse goals, not merely to the dead past but to separate graves.

Quieted by his realization of his own unimportance, in lonely shame and humility Gabriel stretches himself by his sleeping wife and, thinking of his aunts and their approaching death and of all the

dead, he feels the fading of his own identity into vagueness. Looking
westward from the window, watching the snowfall that covers Ireland
with waters frozen to stillness, he feels that "his journey westward"
is imminent. His thoughts carry him to the central plain and hills
and the Bog of Allen, still, turf-colored water, and farther, in transcendence of that stasis, to the Atlantic ocean, "the dark mutinous
Shannon waves" receiving the falling snow. As his soul swoons in
his vision of a universe of snow, Gabriel senses in the oblivion of its
descent the unity of the fate of "all the living and the dead." In
recognizing that fate as universal, his also, Gabriel is restored to the
community of men by his acceptance of the communion of the shades.

Though Gabriel's enlargement and liberation in his final vision is
not a restoration to life, it is an achievement of true dignity and
beauty. The one comparable attainment in *Dubliners* occurs in
"Araby," where the way of release into life, as Joyce conceived it, is
adumbrated in the only action of the book that is creative. By acts of
invention, by transmuting an earthly love in worship and ritual, a boy
attains for a while some measure of religious satisfaction. But his experience is mainly compounded of imaginations and delusory expectations, and he is entirely alone and unsupported. Finding his idol
inadequate to sustain him through all assaults and frustrations, he conceives of no other. He is like Gabriel, the potential artist confined and
disempowered in Dublin.

The spiritual way of escape and attainment, only intimated in
Dubliners, is fully defined in *A Portrait of the Artist as a Young Man,*
in passages not unrelated to these stories. With a priest of the Church
who is merely "schooled in the discharging of a formal rite," Stephen
Dedalus contrasts himself, "a priest of the eternal imagination, transmuting the daily bread of experience into the radiant body of everliving life." The consummate act in the *Portrait* is Stephen's creation
of a work of art. In a series of developments symbolized by images of
generation and of sacred rites amid the cloudy flush and afterglow of
a dream or vision of waves of light, the words of a poem flow into
being in his mind. Here is the process whereby "the uncreated con-
science" of his race will be for d. It is a ritual from which the work
of art emerges, as the consecrated Host emerges from the ritual of
the Mass, to be used for the redemption of the soul from death and
the replenishment of the world with life.

The nature of this most vital action of the soul is made more fully
apparent in the immediately following scene of augury. Watching the
circling flight of swallows, Stephen is reminded of the flight of Daedalus out of captivity, symbol of his own escape from Ireland eastward
over water. In the wanderings of the "birds ever going and coming,
building ever an unlasting home under the eaves of men's houses,"

he seems to find a symbol of constantly renewed creative action and of that ceaseless motion of spirit like endless waters out of which invention comes and which beauty can evoke. Lines of Yeats about the wandering of the swallow over waters stir his life as in an earlier scene it was stirred by a girl—in her power not unlike the Irish madonna of "Araby"—standing beautiful, and birdlike, in midstream, stirring the water of the tide to motion and music. The meaning of that visionary image of beauty in action is disclosed in Stephen's dream that follows in response to it. The dream is of unfolding subjective light, flooding in waves, seeming to be simultaneously a world and a flower and a sea flushing with dawn, a complex of symbolic images like the orient goal of *Dubliners* that has the aspects both of another land than Ireland and of an eastern sea and that is at the same time a state of the soul in fullness of life. The vital condition of the soul thus envisaged is the opposite of the soul's paralysis. It is a state of change in manifold movement, a flowing transmutation of multitudinous form as in the "hitherandthithering waters" of *Finnegans Wake* and in the tidestream stirred by the girl's "foot hither and thither."

Suggestions of such spiritual fulfillment in motion of a subjective light that is like water are to be found in *Dubliners* in Gabriel Conroy's joy, compared to a "wave," and in the images of his past delight that "burst like stars" and "broke upon and illumined his memory" while his illusion held that he and his wife were moving "with wild and radiant hearts to a new adventure." The parallel in the *Portrait* is striking: while Stephen, awaiting the augury, stood repeating the words of Yeats, "a soft liquid joy like the noise of many waters flowed over his memory. . . ." Gabriel's mind, like Stephen's, appears to have been stirring with the promise of life, before he turned to the past, away from the vital east. Perhaps even in the last moments of his decline he might have turned round and moved eastward if his spirit had been stronger. For as "his soul swooned slowly" into the vagueness of the snow and watery darkness, it was being freed of the "nets" of Irish ways, like that of Stephen Dedalus entering the dreamed watery light, whose "soul was swooning into some new world, fantastic, dim, uncertain as under sea. . . . Glimmering and trembling, trembling and unfolding, a breaking light, an opening flower. . . ." Failing to attain the freedom of that light, Gabriel escaped into darkness.

Clearly the escape from Dublin is not to be conceived of finally as a passage beyond physical enclosure, but as a transcendence of psychic constrictions, an attainment of that full motility of the soul which is the reverse of its paralysis. The nature of Joyce's later works of fiction sustains this view. For the scene of all is Dublin, and all develop in one way or another the theme of wholeness in spiritual fullness and freedom. In the character and experience of Leopold Bloom, "all-

roundman," sensitive observer in whom there seems to be "a touch of
the artist," wanderer and "waterlover," the attainment of wholeness
is less approached than suggested. Not alone by Bloom, but in the
very texture of *Ulysses,* is forefigured that universal being embodying
our collective humanity which in *Finnegans Wake* Joyce represented
in the forever renewed activity of a single character in whom all are
comprised. In the interlinking formations and resolutions of meaning
in flow that present the history of this being, Joyce offers to every
reader, if only in the mode of esthetic understanding, a realization of
life integrated in one continuing act of changing and inclusive vision,
a vast epiphany and a communion in which all may share. Thus in
Finnegans Wake the resurrection and the life denied to almost all of
Joyce's characters, found only briefly by the artists and the young, is
discovered in the movement of the everliving spirit of humanity.
Ulysses approached this development. *Dubliners* began it, in a single
symbolic structure consubstantial with a full-bodied naturalistic narrative defining at once the symbolic method of Joyce's successive master-
pieces and the grounds of his mature vision. The revelation thus presented is of the whole moral action of the soul in Dublin moving from
the beginning to the end of its tortuous course between the poles of
life and death.

The Artistry of *Dubliners*

by S. L. Goldberg

Whatever influences may be detected in *Dubliners*—and Chekhov, Maupassant, George Moore, and Flaubert have all been mentioned [1]— and however easy it has since become to write the same kind of stories, it is nevertheless a remarkable achievement for a writer in his early twenties. The stories are by no means simple naturalistic sketches, as some have thought them; nor, on the other hand, are they structures of infinitely complex "symbolism." [2] Each brings a limited area of experience to sharp focus, renders visible its "whatness," and does so with an economical, concentrated purposefulness that gives the realistic details their full metaphorical import. Joyce had learned his craft. What is more, the stories are lightly but suggestively related, so that the book is something more than merely a sum of its parts.

The opening sentences of the first story, "The Sisters," as we gradually come to realise, are something like a statement of the major themes of the whole book:

> There was no hope for him this time: it was the third stroke. Night after night I had passed the house (it was vacation time) and studied the lighted square of the window: and night after night I had found it lighted in the same way, faintly and evenly. If he was dead, I thought, I would see the reflection of candles on the darkened blind, for I knew that two candles must be set at the head of a corpse. He had often said

---

"The Artistry of Dubliners*"* (original title: *"The Development of the Art:* Chamber Music *to* Dubliners*"*). *From* James Joyce *by S. L. Goldberg (Edinburgh: Oliver & Boyd Ltd.; New York: Barnes & Noble, Inc., 1962), pp. 36–46. Copyright © 1962 by S. L. Goldberg. Reprinted by permission of the publishers.*

[1] M. Magalaner and R. M. Kain, *Joyce: the Man, the Work, the Reputation* (New York, 1956), pp. 57 ff.; Alan Tate, "Three Commentaries," *Sewanee Review,* LVIII (1950), p. 1. But cp. Richard Ellmann, *James Joyce* (New York, 1959), p. 171n.

[2] See Magalaner and Kain, *Joyce,* pp. 68 ff. Other "symbolic" explications may be found in B. Ghiselin, "The Unity of Joyce's *Dubliners,*" *Accent,* XVI (1956), pp. 75 ff., 196 ff. [see pp. 57–85 in this volume]; M. Magalaner, *Time of Apprenticeship: The Fiction of the Young James Joyce* (New York, 1959), ch. 3; W. Y. Tindall, *A Reader's Guide to James Joyce* (New York, 1959), ch. 1; but as criticisms of *literature* most of these strike me as either irrelevant or unconvincing.

to me: 'I am not long for this world,' and I had thought his words idle. Now I knew they were true. Every night as I gazed up at the window I said softly to myself the word *paralysis*. It had always sounded strangely in my ears, like the word *gnomon* in the Euclid and the word *simony* in the Catechism. But now it sounded to me like the name of some maleficent and sinful being. It filled me with fear, and yet I longed to be nearer to it and to look upon its deadly work.

The terms "paralysis" and "simony" (more discursively defined in *Stephen Hero*) suggest the pervasive moral condition, the "maleficent and sinful being," exposed in story after story.[3] "Gnomon" suggests their artistic method, by which the whole is suggested by the part or (as with the gnomon on a sun-dial) the light by its shadow: the simple but effective metaphor of light/darkness is used in many of the stories.

In this first story, the old priest's physical paralysis becomes the mark of his failure of courage before the divine mystery he had tried to serve, and of his consequent resignation to hopelessness and death. In "An Encounter," the paralysis is that of diseased obsession. The unruly, romantic, adventurous spirit of the boy, seeking a larger freedom of life, encounters only the maleficent disorder of the old pervert; yet although he fears it, he outwits it: courage wins him his freedom. In "Araby," the boy's romantic longings at last collapse and yet triumph in the darkened hall of the bazaar; the chink of money and the inane chatter there come to represent the materialistic "simony" which (even in his own desires) at once betrays his foolish ideals and is itself exposed by their innocent "folly." And so on through the book. The stories become images: of paralysed automatism of the will, the paralysing hand of the past, a paralysing feebleness of moral imagination, a simoniacal willingness to buy and sell the life of the spirit, timidity, frustration, self-righteousness, fear of convention, fear of sin, hypocrisy, vulgarity, pettiness. Each, with a fine dexterity, vivisects its material to lay bare the moral disease that distorts it to its present shape.

The metaphor of vivisection is Joyce's own,[4] and it describes perfectly the art of such stories as "Two Gallants" or "Ivy Day in the Committee Room" or "Grace," an art swift, sharp, accurate, with every stroke deliberately measured. The tone is flat, grimly reticent; the style distant; the observation and metaphorical detail so consistently pointed that they achieve a kind of wit. Yet the success is not consistent. Some stories are too intent upon their analytical purposes. The formal neatness of "Eveline," "After the Race," "The Boarding House," and "Counterparts," for instance, is so obvious and oversimplifying, that the art comes to seem almost programmatic. These stories lack the vital detail

[3] Cp. A. Ostroff, "The Moral Vision in *Dubliners*," *Western Speech*, XX (1956), pp. 196 ff.

[4] *Stephen Hero* (New York, 1955), p. 186.

pressing *against* the author's scalpel, and they also lack the author's rather malicious enjoyment both of his material and of his skill in dealing with it, which enliven "Two Gallants," "Ivy Day," "Grace," or even "A Little Cloud," "Clay," and "A Mother." But then, as all these images of spiritual decay succeed each other, we may well begin to question the mood of the book generally. Is not its tone, indeed its whole attitude to life, perhaps too insistently, and too constrictingly, "vivisective"?

Our answer inevitably reflects our view of Joyce's work as a whole. To some critics, *Dubliners* is a dispassionate, morally realistic account of modern life, Joyce's discovery of his lifelong attitude (ironical exposure) to his lifelong subject ("paralysis" and alienation). To others, his irony is "romantic," built upon the contrast between the individual's desires or feelings and the sordid realities of the modern world. To others again, his irony is only a device (like Chekhov's) for heightening the pity and terror of life.[5] Clearly, there are grounds for each of these judgments; but we also have to remember Joyce's relative immaturity when he wrote *Dubliners* and not be surprised if the book betrays it. Even while recognising the artistic success, we must also appreciate its limitations—not least because both help to explain Joyce's further development. And, not unnaturally, the limitations are very much those revealed more blatantly in *Stephen Hero*: an uncertain grasp of the values by which others are criticised, a vagueness about the genuine "life" by which simony and paralysis are constantly measured, a tendency to oversimplify reality in the process of exposing it.

It is not that the stories fail to imply the importance of courage, self-knowledge, fulfilment, freedom, or even the plainer domestic virtues; nor do they lack pity of a kind. But the comparison with Chekhov (or *Ulysses* for that matter) shows how little these values mean in *Dubliners,* how little it reveals what they might *be* in the actual experience of ordinary people, how complacent is its superior viewpoint. Some of the stories do reach towards a more self-critical, more specific, and hence (to that degree) deeper insight: "Araby," for example, "The Boarding House," "A Painful Case," and (most notably) "The Dead" —each, incidentally, the last in its respective group (childhood, adolescence, maturity, and public life).[6] But "Araby," for all its tone of mature wisdom, remains slightly evasive about how compromised the boy's romanticism really is; "The Boarding House" can only gesture vaguely towards the interconnexions between the mother's "simoniacal" plotting and the possibilities of life opening before her daughter as a

[5] *E.g.* Hugh Kenner, *Dublin's Joyce* (Bloomington, 1955), ch. 5 [see pp. 38–56 in this volume]; Harry Levin, *James Joyce: A Critical Introduction* (Norfolk, 1960), p. 41; Magalaner and Kain, *Joyce,* p. 62.

[6] Ellmann, *James Joyce,* p. 216.

result, symbolically suggesting only enough to make us realise how little the art realises (here and elsewhere) of the complicating paradoxes of life.

"A Painful Case" takes a rather longer step towards maturity. The stories immediately preceding it reveal an obvious pity for the frustrated lives they portray, but as Joyce's imagination is devoted less to the individual character than to the kind of situation he represents, so the pity is somewhat aloof, superior to its human object. "A Painful Case" deals with a related but deeper emotion: compassion. As many have pointed out, it portrays what Joyce felt he himself might have been (the central character, Mr Duffy, is actually modelled on Stanislaus);[7] it is also like a self-comment on the tone of much of *Dubliners*. For Mr Duffy is locked, irretrievably, in the hell of his egocentric superiority to life. He refuses ordinary conventions and even ordinary carnal love; he disdains "to live, to err, to fall," and therefore, despite his literary pretensions, can never "triumph, . . . recreate life out of life."[8] Only the shock of Mrs Sinico's destruction enables him to see anything of his "paralysis," and then only partially and too late. The ending of the story illustrates perfectly what Joyce's art could achieve at this stage and what it could not. The recumbent figures in the park, where Mr Duffy stands at night, are still merely "venal and furtive loves" for him, though he despairs at his own loveless state. The subtle identification of the man and the "obstinate" and "laborious" engine disappearing into the darkness, his lapsing sense of reality, the perfectly silent darkness in which he feels himself alone, are precisely right. Nevertheless, the repeated phrase—"outcast from life's feast"—remains, as it must in the very terms in which the situation is observed, only the merest "symbol" of a life fuller and richer than his "rectitude" or the "venal and furtive loves" (117). The story gives it no more positive meaning than that. And what applies to "eating" here applies to a great many other "symbols" earnestly explicated by Joyce's critics; they are all *too* "suggestive" and therefore vague, too undefined dramatically. We could say that by choosing to work through the limited consciousness of his characters, Joyce found the best way to make their limitations imaginatively real, and thus avoided the need to define *his* position, to give meaning to his own stance in or behind the narrative, except by oblique "symbols" of the relevant values. We could equally well say that while he had no fuller sense of those values than he shows here, he simply could not see more in his characters than their limitations. The strength of *Dubliners* is the formal clarity, the subtlety and precision of its art—qualities that derive partly from a finely-sustained

[7] Stanislaus Joyce, *My Brother's Keeper* (New York, 1958), p. 165; cp. Ellmann, *James Joyce*, p. 39.

[8] *A Portrait of the Artist as a Young Man* (New York, 1928), p. 200.

discipline but partly also from an immaturity of insight that made the
formal problems relatively simple. Perhaps the most striking thing
about the book, indeed, is the way Joyce turned his very limitations to
account.

"The Dead," the last of the stories and the last written, is, I believe,
the exception that proves the rule. It has been universally admired,
and it is a minor masterpiece in its own right.[9] One important difference from the other stories is its protagonist. Gabriel Conroy is an
intelligent and complex man, and Joyce's art is now at last capable of
portraying him as such. In many ways he, too, represents a self Joyce
might have been: a university teacher, a "man of letters" in a minor
way, critical of Irish provincialism, sensitive to its frustrations—" 'O,
to tell the truth, . . . I'm sick of my own country, sick of it!' " (189).
That sickness is diagnosed very subtly, and a second important difference from the other stories is the kind of irony that emerges. For there
are no simple black-and-white judgments here, but rather a delicate
balancing of insights. In fact, that balance is the story's central theme,
and it heralds the spirit of Joyce's major works.

Gabriel's "sickness" is partly that he aspires to the wider and more
vital possibilities he sees in Europe; partly that his education makes
him feel morally superior to others; partly that he is unable to imagine
others' lives sympathetically, so that a touch of egocentricity mars all
his personal relations and all his judgments. At his aunts' annual party
he is a favoured and admired guest, but he shows himself awkward,
slightly pompous, inclined to resent others and to impose on them his
own attitudes and his own good opinion of himself. Yet beneath all
this lies an uncertainty, a genuine goodwill, and at bottom a saving
humility. During the party a number of little frustrations jar his self-
esteem. His impulse is to retreat: out of the tangled involvements of
life to the clean, abstract, simple, and solitary world of the snow
outside (192; 202). Significantly, we are made to perceive the bracing
vigour which attracts him from the room, with its decaying echoes of
once-vital social customs, as well as his evasion of the actual life the
room contains. He is revealed as the victim of his self-ignorance. Ironically, the drunkard he despises proves capable of a spontaneous grace
he could never manage (193); he misses the ironical application to
himself of his story about the old horse who could not break the habit
of the treadmill (208); ironically, he cannot appreciate his own speech
toasting his aunts. To him they are "only two ignorant old women"

[9] Cp. David Daiches, *The Novel and the Modern World* (Chicago, 1960), pp.
73 ff. [see pp. 32–37 in this volume]; Tate in *Sewanee Review* (1950); Ellmann,
James Joyce, pp. 252 ff.; Ghiselin, in *Accent* (1956), pp. 207–11; Kenner, *Dublin's
Joyce*, pp. 62–8; Magalaner and Kain, *Joyce*, pp. 92–8 (though the last two seem
to me to distort various aspects of the story).

(192)—like the old horse. What he says out of a mean and self-protective impulse expresses, beneath its sentimentality, a deeper truth than he realises: that traditions do live on and yet die, that life is choked and haunted by the dead and yet goes on. "We have all of us living duties and living affections which claim, and rightly claim, our strenuous endeavours. Therefore, I will not linger on the past . . ." (204). The vividly evoked scene, the tangled relationships, the dramatically controlled symbolism, are created by a style now so responsive that it seems to disappear into the drama itself.

When Gabriel sees his wife on the stairs listening to an old ballad he asks himself what she is a symbol of. "*Distant Music* he would call the picture if he were a painter" (210). And being the man he is, he takes the music and its strange effect on her for his own. Suddenly he desires her, impatiently, thinking of their long intimacy together, alone, living in the "cold" with their mutual flame: "Like distant music these words that he had written years before were borne towards him from the past. He longed to be alone with her" (214). In truth, "he longed to be master of her strange mood" (217). The last shattering blow to his complacency is the truth about her mood—that it is not for him but the memory of a young man she had known years before, who had sung that ballad and who had died, in the brightness of his passionate love, for her. Gabriel is not insensitive; he sees his own egotism; but the "shameful consciousness of his own person" that now floods over him is not (as it is sometimes taken to be) the climactic moment of insight. It is only the reverse side of his egotism. He is no more merely a "ludicrous figure," a "nervous, well-meaning sentimentalist . . . idealizing his own clownish lusts," a "pitiable fatuous fellow," than his fellow-Dubliners are merely ignorant and foolish, drunkards, moral paralytics, mere gibbering ghosts of the past. One of the dramatic triumphs of the story is that we realise already what Gabriel must come to realise, know already what his listening wife was a symbol of. For a moment Gabriel nearly fails, and the moment, though dramatically unstressed, is a crucial act of self-criticism on Joyce's part:

'I think he died for me,' she answered.
A vague terror seized Gabriel at this answer, as if, at that hour when he had hoped to triumph, some impalpable and vindictive being was coming against him, gathering forces against him in its vague world. But he shook himself free of it with an effort of reason and continued to caress her hand. . . . (220)

The sense of some *external* evil, some "maleficent and sinful being," threatening the inviolate self—the assumption that dominates and limits the stories from the very first page—is here at last purged. Reason and love, an unspectacular but visibly "unresentful" and "generous" love, replace it; the veiled kinetic "riot" of self-defensive emotion gives way to a real *stasis* of spirit. And only now is Gabriel free, able to feel what the whole story has enacted: the complex tangle of distance and presence, passion and decay, love and detachment, aspiration and limit, life and death, in every individual and every society. The snow no longer represents to him the purity of the withdrawn self; as he "swoons" into unconsciousness, it seems to fall "like the descent of their last end, upon all the living and the dead" (224).

This story has often been compared with *Exiles* because of the personal and marital issues treated in both.[10] In more fundamental ways, however, it is prophetic of the end of *Ulysses*, where Leopold Bloom reaches at last a similar moral *stasis*; and perhaps also prophetic—in its rather equivocal "swooning" into the snow-world, a vast, undifferentiating state beyond all life and death—of *Finnegans Wake* as well. The swelling release of emotion is here just kept in control; with Molly Bloom and in *Finnegans Wake* it is more elaborately disguised and escapes. But "The Dead" is finally unshaken. Its deeply felt conviction, its originality, the range and subtlety of its drama, its complex yet assured ironies, its humility before life, place it apart from the rest of *Dubliners*. Fine as they are, the other stories stand judged by this. In the six or seven years from the early poems, Joyce virtually found himself as a writer.

---

[10] *E.g.* Levin, *James Joyce*, p. 43; Kenner, *Dublin's Joyce*, pp. 68–9.

"Araby" and the "Extended Simile"

By Ben L. Collins

"Araby," the third story in *Dubliners,* is the final tale of the phase of childhood (a sort of Telemachiad), and, as such, rightfully sums up the whole of that phase of the moral paralysis the heart of which Joyce feels to lie in Dublin. (The other phases of course are adolescence, maturity, and public life.) It is a peculiarity of *Dubliners* that each main character introduced carries not only his own burden, but also the compounded burdens of those characters who have preceded him. It is so with the unnamed boy of "Araby," though he carries on his back his own accumulated experiences.

It is not difficult to see, therefore, how religion in the form of the dead priest and the broken chalice of "The Sisters"; how adventure, romance, and religion in the form of the uncompleted trip to the Pigeonhouse of "An Encounter"; and how the quest for the father surrogate in both stories are carried over into "Araby," where their combined efforts will make the necessary impact upon the young hero as yet unaware of the real and all-embracing lack in his world and life—the void in which all attempts at beauty, love, faith, and belonging will be frustrated. In short, the symbols which are clear to the reader have not yet communicated themselves to the lad. It is interesting to note that after "Araby" Joyce changes the point-of-view; he shifts from first person to third. It is as if all has been said, the thesis made. All that is needed is documentation. Now the artist like a god can stand outside, above, and beyond his work, looking down, paring his fingernails.

Because of its seeming simplicity, "Araby" has been looked upon by commentators—some of whom, to be sure, have noted the possibility of complexity—as concerned essentially with illusion and reality, as a so-called initiation story in which the protagonist moves from ignorance to knowledge, from innocence to the brink of maturity. And of course they are correct: we do learn along with the boy that there is nothing to hope for in his world, that there are nets flung at the

---

" 'Araby' and the 'Extended Simile' " (original title: "Joyce's 'Araby' and the 'Extended Simile' ") by Ben L. Collins. From James Joyce Quarterly, *IV (Winter, 1967), 84–90. Reprinted by permission of Thomas F. Staley, Editor.*

soul of a man born in his country that keep him back from flight. But to read it only in this light, to leave a story as potentially great as this one with only the idea that "love" or the "romantic life" cannot be supported in paralytic Dublin and the sooner one knows it the better is to miss most of its richness and nearly all of the fun. For in doing so we disregard the quintessence of Joyce's artistry—his ability to build layer upon layer of meaning without detriment to the literal level of the story.

In order to introduce what I am about to say—perhaps to justify the approach—I have unconscionably added to the plethora of literary terms one of my own: Extended Simile. By extended simile I mean a figure that *likens* one thing to another but which does not *equate*. Unlike the simile or the epic simile which compares descriptively, the extended simile affects the total meaning of a work. While the extended metaphor creates allegory, the extended simile can allegorize for a moment and then liken the same thing to something else. By means of this diversification, one object can operate on several levels at the same time, and allow parallel, allusion, and quasi-allegorical elements to become operative once or many times with one or many meanings— allow the author to *suggest* without statement, allegory, or heavy-handed symbolism.

To illustrate: near the beginning of "Araby" is a sentence seemingly innocent and inserted between others perhaps to belie its importance:

> The wild garden behind the house contained a central apple tree and a few straggling bushes under one of which I found the late tenant's rusty bicycle pump.*

The central apple tree and the rusty bicycle pump obviously are important to the story. They *liken* the yard to the Garden of Eden, but there seems no suggestion that the entire story is an allegory of man's fall from grace—or is there? The rusty bicycle pump becomes only vaguely and temporarily the Serpent in the Garden. And yet the meaning of the story is foreshadowed by these objects. Perhaps the best example of the use of extended simile is Mangan's sister; she shall be treated fully in a moment.

Let us go back briefly to the contention that "Araby" is an initiation story concerned primarily with appearance and reality. The word *blind,* then, is of course essential to an interpretation: "North Richmond Street, being blind. . . ." that is, a dead-end street; the window blind behind which the boy watches for Mangan's sister; and the implication of previous blindness—much like the idea in Oedipus—at the end, "Gazing up into the darkness I saw myself as a creature driven and derided by vanity; and my eyes burned with anguish and anger." Certainly this is one of Joyce's ways of introducing the obliquities to follow. The dead-end street tells that any quest in Dublin will lead to a dead-end, an impasse. The idea of love's being blind and that the blindness of the illusion leads to a view of darkness when the reality becomes apparent resolve the paradox of the final lines.

The idea of blindness to reality continues in the children's sense of well-being, unaware that they, like Eden, are, outside their patch of ever-changing violet sky toward which the feeble rays of the lamps reach, surrounded by dripping gardens, ashpits, odorous stables as well as by shadows under whose protection the boy may hide from uncle and true love.

The colors brown and yellow, Joyce's colors for decay, predominate: the houses gaze at each other with brown imperturbable faces, Mangan's sister's brown figure, the yellowed pages of *The Memoirs of Vidoq*. Even the winter season and the bitter, wet weather preclude a bright outcome. The above, though they function basically as foreshadowings, are enough to set the tone and regulate understanding, and it is generally through these and the literal level of the story that "Araby" is interpreted.

The central apple tree, as suggested earlier, is one of the important elements of the work, for in bringing to mind the Garden of Eden it introduces two of the story's basic motifs—love and religion. The Garden is connotative both of man's fall and women: Adam through his love for Eve ate of the fruit of the Tree of Knowledge and was cast from Paradise into the world of reality. This allusion or quasi-allegory describes what is yet to happen in "Araby."

The rusty bicycle pump, peeping out from under an adjacent bush like the Serpent in the Garden, suggests that like it love and religion which could once inflate (raise and elate) are inoperative and relates directly to its late owner, the dead priest.

But it is to Mangan's sister that we must turn to find the focal image of the story. She is, after all, the object of the boy's affection, and like him she is purposefully unnamed. Through her Joyce can sum up and indicate the true breadth of the moral paralysis. She represents Church (in that she includes Christ, Mary, and the priesthood), Ireland, and the betrayer Judas.

That she is *Mangan's* sister, that she has no other name than Mangan, forces the reader to dwell upon that name. Those informed will be minded of the Irish poet James Clarence Mangan, said to be an inspiration to the Irish movement but nevertheless admired by Joyce and the subject of an early essay by him in *St. Stephen's*. To the world, Mangan is known, if at all, for his "The Dark Rosaleen," a translation and adaptation of an old Irish poem. Though seemingly a poem of love, the work is an allegory in which a hero (Hugh the Red O'Donnell) is coming to save Ireland (the Dark Rosaleen) from the Saxons (the English) who are besetting her. The men of God (Church and Pope) are also on their way with help and gifts to raise Ireland from her inglorious position. By allusion to this poem, the themes of love and religion are re-enforced and the theme of nationality—about which Joyce has already concerned himself by mention of the come-all-you's of O'Donovan Rossa and the ballads about the troubles of the country —is introduced. Modern Ireland is in a like situation, beset by England and in need of a hero. The role of Mangan's sister as deity is made known, if it cannot establish itself in any other way, comically, for one little knows Joyce who feels that he was unaware of or incapable of using Mangan's initials—J.C.

But mere allusion in this case is not enough; there must be comment, however recondite. In his hopeless love for Mangan's sister, the boy reverts to his experiences of the two earlier stories, bringing into play the idea of *quest* and the *chalice*. His love intensifies the illusion that the world has romantic and religious content, and he can go through the sordid streets bearing, but not dropping, his imaginary grail. He is the knight errant, the courtly lover, coursing through throngs of imaginary foes in places "hostile to romance"—where patriotic songs are sung—as well as Mariolater where the "shrill litanies of shopboys" are heard and whence "her name sprang to my lips at moments in strange prayers and praises which I myself did not understand."

When finally he speaks to her, she stands above him, holding a spike of the porch railing, in the high position he has accorded her. At this moment we are to see her through the boy's eyes as the kind of love which refines itself from the physical to the sublime—like Dante's love for Beatrice in *La Vita Nuova* and the *Commedia*—a love able to transcend the mundane, manifest itself in the abstract, and finally resolve itself in the fervent religious intensity necessary for union with God. The boy feels that Mangan's sister is that purifying force standing above him like God or Mary or as a priest offering him the wafer of communion. (It is possible now to see the economy employed in the titles of the dead priest's books: the boy is *The Devout Communicant*; she *The Abbot*; and the result will be the theft of the illusion, for Vidoq was a thief.) The boy fails to see, however, what should now be clear to the reader, that the description of Magnan's sister informs against her, that it will ultimately keep the love and its ramifications earthbound. The girl's "holiness" is marred not only by the "spike" she holds but also by her show of neck and petticoat, the hanging rope (noose) of her hair, and her brown garb (Beatrice wore white). By these and by the silver bracelet which she turns round and round her wrist, she is seen to be earthly and material. (She can be compared to and contrasted with Stephen Dedalus' "vision" in *A Portrait of the Artist as a Young Man* which gave to him a "profane" joy and led him from religion to art.) Her noose of hair and her silver bracelet strongly urge a consideration of a recurrent motif in Joyce— the betrayal-crucifixion. The bracelet may be likened to Judas' silver, the rope to the crucifixion, the death of the illusion. It is she who suggests the bazaar that she cannot herself attend because of a religious *retreat*, and it is there that the boy has his awakening and discovers that he is part and parcel of his own betrayal. Joyce's constant building seems to indicate that he was not content to show the paralysis on one level only.

Because the narrative is concerned with "puppy" love, and because woman is the immediate object of the quest, it may be well to examine the other women in the story (as well as one man) to determine whether they too play a part in the boy's ultimate disillusionment. That the first three stories of *Dubliners* depict a boy who resides with an aunt and uncle is reason enough for the quest-father surrogate motifs. Although there is no evidence that he is treated unkindly, he is not treated tenderly: the uncle answers him curtly and then causes him to be late for the bazaar; the aunt, though finally she stands up for him, is less than sympathetic. Mrs. Mercer, the garrulous widow of a pawn-broker who collects stamps for some pious purpose, has her impact on him. But it is the young woman at the bazaar with her retort, "Oh, there's a fib" (a clear Joycean epiphany; she withholds the word *lie* because it isn't genteel), who is the instrument of his final under-standing and its concomitant anguish and anger.

So it is Mangan's sister who has sent him off to Araby, his uncle who has made him later, and his aunt and Mrs. Mercer with whom he has spent part of the interval. His mood of the evening has changed from anticipation to distress. The exotic name of the affair could not but have awakened anticipation in so sensitive a person; indeed, even his prosaic uncle is impelled to recite "The Arab's Farewell to His Steed," the poem itself serving as a foreshadowing if the boy is likened to the Arab, the steed to Romance. But the lateness of the hour, the expensive entrance he must choose, and the half-dark bazaar have primed him for his final realization. The almost empty hall reminds him of a church after the celebrants and communicants have left— something of the Chapel Perilous of the Grail legends; the clink of coins—reminiscent of the money-changers in the temple—stir him to an awareness of the crass, material real world which, deluded, he could previously ignore; the shabbiness of his surroundings removes from him the aura of romance; and the girl's retort, "Oh, there's a fib," informs him that his illusion is a "fib," that vanity had obfuscated the reality which has now become apparent. He can no longer carry his chalice through places hostile to romance, and, like Father Flynn, drops it in despair. All of the themes are brought together again here, but they are now understood. The boy has moved from childhood, but his new knowledge—consider now the central apple tree—brings him neither joy nor great expectations.

Two more ideas need examining, however, before we have exhausted the possibilities of the story and the scope of Joyce's plan—and then one can never be sure. In *Ulysses* Joyce parallels his work to Homer's *The Odyssey* and, perhaps to a lesser extent, to Dante's *Commedia*. These parallels may also be seen to work in *Dubliners*; the former has been demonstrated by Richard Levin and Charles Shattuck to appear in the stories. The following outlines that section concerned with "Araby." [1]

The parallel here is concerned primarily with Book III of *The Odyssey*, the final section of the Telemachiad, which finds Telemachus at the palace of Menelaus and Helen inquiring after his father. The boy of "Araby" becomes Telemachus in search of a father—here a father substitute—and the women in the *Dubliners* story converge to become Helen, who, in her tale of contemplated perfidy, becomes the destroyer of men. Both tales end without satisfying their protagonists, both end on notes of near despair.

The role of the Commedia is less clear in "Araby" than it is in another of the stories. In "Grace" we have an obvious parallel of hell, purgatory, and heaven in Mr. Kernan's fall down the stairs into the lavatory of the pub, his recuperation, and his presence at the businessmen's retreat in the *Gardiner* Street Church where he sits in quincunx formation with his four friends and hears the sermon of a worldly priest.

In "Araby," the allusion, though less sure, is used to a more serious end. Like Dante, the boy has strayed: his schoolmaster wonders if he has begun to idle; his aunt feels him capable of attending a Freemason's affair. Like Dante, too, the boy has idealized a Beatrice. [2] He has strayed

---

[1] Richard Levin and Charles Shattuck, "First Flight to Ithaca," *Accent* (Winter, 1944).

[2] But the approaches to the idealized woman are diametrically opposed: Dante (we are led to believe from *La Vita Nuova*) approached Beatrice *from* the romantic, courtly aspect of love *to* a divine personification of her; the boy in "Araby" sees Mangan's sister first as divine and then recognizes that his interest is really romantic.

from the path, but it is not until the evening of the bazaar when his singing changes to fear and foreboding that *he* has any feeling of impending disaster. Having finally arrived at Araby, he enters through the turnstile—not the first instance of the "circle" idea—and pays his shilling (he has started with a *florin*) as though to Charon. In the manner of Dante's damned souls who know the past and future but not the present, the boy cannot remember why he has come.

During this lapse, the symbolism suddenly changes. What previously passed for pure love is now shown to be sensual. The imagery, the idea of the grail, the jars and teapots, the empty hall itself—even the remembrance of the empty house of two storeys at the blind end of North Richmond Street—have changed, have turned into female sexual symbols. (If Joyce did not know Freud or Frazer, surely he knew Wolfram von Eschenbach and Gottfried von Strassburg or other analogues of *Parzifal* and *Tristan*.) He has deluded himself as to the nature of his love; the divine love he thought he felt for Mangan's sister was really passion, but a passion so new to him, perhaps, that he did not recognize it. It was really the show of throat and petticoat that entranced him; there is no other love in Joyce's book.

Yet this is not merely puberty rearing its ugly head. The midpoint of life is not one half of three score and ten, but the point between childhood and maturity. In both the *Commedia* and "Araby" the midpoint has to do with the (central) garden—note that in "Grace" Kernan approaches the divine in the *Gardiner* Street Church; that is, the garden lies midway between the lowest part of hell (Satan) and the highest part of heaven (God). For Dante, whose love is no longer of this world, the Garden is the point of ascension for purged souls; for Joyce, because the Garden is inoperative and because love has not been refined, one is cast into the hell of the world of reality. It is only an illusion that love exists, and because love is the only saving grace, when it falls all that is positive falls with it. There is, then, no heaven for the Dubliner, for here the human spirit has been entrapped.

"Two Gallants" and "Ivy Day in the Committee Room"

by Robert Boyle, S. J.

The central image of Joyce's "Two Gallants," as I interpret it, is that of the exposed, heedless, weary harp, whose mournful music struck silent the two Dublin gallants:

> Not far from the porch of the club a harpist stood in the roadway, playing to a little ring of listeners. He plucked at the wires heedlessly, glancing quickly from time to time at the face of each new-comer and from time to time, wearily also, at the sky. His harp, too, heedless that her coverings had fallen about her knees, seemed weary alike of the eyes of strangers and of her master's hands. One hand played in the bass the melody of *Silent, O Moyle,* while the other hand careered in the treble after each group of notes. The notes of the air sounded deep and full.

Moore's poem expresses the paralyzing charm cast upon Lir's daughter, the symbol of poor, paralyzed, charmed Ireland:

> Silent, oh Moyle, be the roar of the water,
> Break not, ye breezes, your chain of repose,
> While, murmuring mournfully, Lir's lonely daughter
> Tells to the night-star her tale of woes . . .
> Yet still in her darkness doth Erin lie sleeping,
> Still doth the pure light its dawning delay . . .

Joyce's image of the harp with her coverings about her knees suggests Moore's handling of this symbol of Ireland, striking in Joyce's apparently naturalistic and matter-of-fact context. It recalls, among other things, Moore's "Sing, Sweet Harp," his desire to recall through the harp the

> . . . vanished fame,
> Whose light once round us shone;
> Of noble pride, now turned to shame,

"'Two Gallants' and 'Ivy Day in the Committee Room'" by Robert Boyle, S. J. From James Joyce Quarterly, I (Fall, 1963), 3–9. Reprinted by permission of Thomas F. Staley, Editor.

And hopes for ever gone . . .
How mournfully the midnight **air**
Among thy chords doth sigh,
As if it sought some echo there
Of voices long gone by;—
Of Chieftains, now forgot, who seemed
The foremost then in fame . . .

Joyce's harp is mournful too, and its mournful music follows the two gallants and binds them to silence. They are listening, surely, to some echo sounding in those deep and full notes. One of these gallants is, after all, the son of a well-known and respected Chieftain (if only an inspector of police; where else could Dublin find remnants of her romantic kings?).

With this image of the harp as fulcrum, the chiasmic structure of the simple, deeply significant action of the story achieves its balance. As Corley moves up to the money paid him by the slavey, he moves down at the same time to the ultimate degradation of a gallant, the absolute denial of the romantic ideal. And in both aspects of his act, he is the "base betrayer," not only of his own potentially gallant manhood, but of Ireland as represented in him. The naked harp is weary, mournful, and hopeless with reason, since in Corley we see her ignored, despised, and sold for a gold coin.

The faint glimmering of gallantry that did actually exist in Corley at one time dies completely in the light from the gold coin. This is symbolized in the story, I think, by the gradual fading of the faint romantic moon, its complete disappearance behind the rain-clouds, and its replacement by the shining gold coin.

Corley is not the only important figure, of course. Lenehan is equally important, if not more so. It is the relationship between the two men that counts. As the song of the harp looks back to an honorable and romantic past, so the relationship between Corley and Lenehan looks back to that which once existed between knight and squire.

Corley fulfills the role of knight in many ways: he is the experienced and successful jouster, the Byronic gay Lothario *in extremis;* he is, in the egotistic reporting of his forensic victories, the Florentine (not only romantically, but in a Machiavellian sense too, since he is the dogmatic teacher of his "disciple"); like former knights pricking on the plain, he seeks "adventure"; his stiff and formal gait, with the *necessity* of moving his body from the hips, suggests, if not armor, at least ritual; and he is "class," not to be got on the inside of, confident of victory and worthy of the admiration and emulation of his squire.

Lenehan, while he is with Corley, skips and peers in spite of his grey hair and ravaged look; he imitates as he can the dress of a torea-

dor (or a squire); he is "armed with a vast stock of stories"; he is servile
and flattering, giving a precious cigarette to the man who spiritually
rapes him (at least that seems to be the source of his ravaged look and
the causality behind his restlessness when away from Corley, his thinking of the harp and its songs, and his spiritual relief and hope); he
follows and admires and hopes to imitate Corley in finding "some good
simpleminded girl with a little of the ready"; he walks aimlessly when
he is away from Corley (the harp's melody controls his movements, but
he has no other goal than that which Corley represents), and discusses
with other young men (other squires?) the money-making schemes of
the more dominant figures (other knights?); he too has class, an air of
gentility which he tries to disguise in the restaurant; and he is a
disciple, who in the end finds as his goal not the moon which attracted
his earnest gaze at the beginning of the story, but the shining gold coin
in the palm of his master.

The girl, a necessary but minor figure, is the lady-fair, "the fine
decent tart," who best serves such gallants. Since she must double as
the lady to be served and the enemy to be conquered (. . . "are you
sure you can bring it off all right?"), it is fortunate that she is stout,
muscular, and healthy. She wears the colors symbolic of the Blessed
Virgin and is of course not betrayed. Actually she shares in the betrayal
of the weary sad harp (whose voice, though, she does not hear) in her
unmalicious, almost instinctive impurity.

The following diagram attempts to outline the double movement
central in the story:

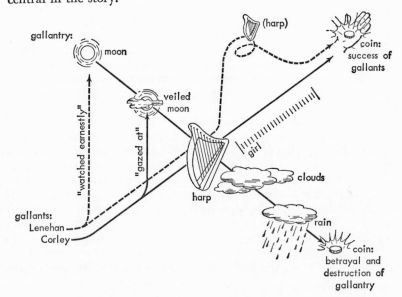

Corley goes straight to his goal, with Lenehan beside him as they pass the harp. Both of them are bound by the spell of the harp (for both must be "released" by the lights and crowd), but to no effect. Corley is not caused to swerve by the implicit appeal of the harp (which is the appeal of romantic, gallant Ireland), because he is the *knight* of ungallantry. Lenehan, the squire, the learner, is less insensitive, but he is content to play the air with his padded, restless, aimless feet; he is too "dry" to respond. The end of the story finds them both gazing at the gold coin which represents the goal of their dreams, the crown of their conception of gallantry.

But they are aware of what they are doing, if not with full consciousness. The effect of the harp brings out that point. Further, there is the imagery of light emanating from jewels and especially from the moon. The lamps in the opening paragraph are "like illumined pearls" for some romantic lady-fair, and the "large faint moon" upon which Lenehan fixes his gaze (while Corley smiles at passing girls) is "circled with a double halo," lovely if seemingly weary like Sidney's sad moon. Lenehan "watched earnestly the passing of the grey web of twilight across its face." That earnestness rises, surely, from the shadow of some inner web of twilight veiling the ideal which poets have always found well symbolized by the moon.

Even Corley "gazed at the pale disc of the moon, now nearly veiled . . ." But he is licking his chops at the time, and that frail shadow of romantic love will be swallowed totally in the darkness of unnatural profiteering. That darkness is almost at hand, and the weary harpist gazes at the "sky" merely, for the moon is by this time veiled in clouds. The moon is thoroughly gone at the end; there is even rain, which Lenehan takes as a warning. Perhaps the significance of that warning, besides the obvious warning to hurry and join Corley before the full rain fell, is that he should hurry himself to find shelter from the clouds of age, aimlessness, and frustration. At any rate, he does find a possibly significant light to attract his earnest gaze in the ritually extended palm of the knight who has achieved the gleaming golden grail of modern Dublin's gallants.

Light flows from a poem upon the souls of patriots and politicians in Joyce's "Ivy Day in the Committee Room." The theme of this story, according to MM. Levin and Shattuck ("First Flight to Ithaca: A New Reading of Joyce's Dubliners," in *james joyce: two decades of criticism*, edited by Seon Givens), parallels that of Books 13–16 of the *Odyssey* —"the nation sick with longing for the return of its lost leader." Whether or not Joyce intends such a *parallel*, which seems to me doubtful, that is certainly the theme, particularly if one takes the word "sick" at its full literal value.

In regard to the details of the story, however, Levin and Shattuck are less successful in establishing a meaningful parallel between this story and the *Odyssey*. They have old Jack related to Eumaeus, which misleads, since old Jack is neither loyal to Parnell nor active in his service. Tierney as the wooers, Colgan as Telemachus, the party workers as the servants of Odysseus's house, and Joe Hynes as the disguised Odysseus and the goddess Athene—these are suggestive and stimulating parallels, but not altogether accurate, as I hope to indicate in my discussion. To link the beer-boy with Mesaulius and Father Keon with Theoclymenus seems to me rather ingenious than helpful.

Joyce is, however, like Homer in at least one way. He builds his story with the apparently effortless mastery of the great artist. His characters are not symbols in any narrowly artificial or contrived sense. If they achieve symbolic stature, it is because they are human beings completely and profoundly realized. If they tell more than their own personal story (as they certainly do—they tell the story of Ireland), it is because they bring their environment with them. The story that unfolds before us does not in any significant way spring from Homer's poem, but grows out of these Irish persons and their relations with one another.

We see old Jack trying to keep warmth in the dark room by raking the cinders. A figure of decay he is, weakened by drink, disappointed and despised at home, worried too (as he shows in his disapproval of Henchy's giving a drink to the beer-boy) about his own son's tendency to follow his example.

O'Connor, grey-haired in his youth, and blotchy, performs a symbolic action in burning Tierney's card to light his cigarette. And the light from that burning card lights up Parnell's ivy in his coat. The contrast between the destructive and vicious politics revealed in the story, and the life-giving forces represented by the ivy, could scarcely be more dramatically emphasized. If his heart is in Glasnevin, where Parnell lies buried, what is he doing here?

Hynes answers the question almost immediately by asking, "Has he paid you yet?" Hynes is the loyal man, the only one who wears his ivy leaf honestly. He supports Colgan, of course, because like Parnell, Colgan works against special interests and against England.

Henchy (the suggested repulsive diminutive points to his character, as did "Corley," little heart, in "Two Gallants") is the true villain of this story, the hypocrite whose lips speak fairly to all and whose heart rots in its self-absorption. He takes the old man's chair while protesting against his moving; he criticizes Tierney to Hynes, but condemns Hynes (in his absence) for lack of "loyalty" to Tierney; he is polite to Keon, gives a drink to the boy, kow-tows to the self-satisfied and superior Crofton (in his presence). Like all truly evil men, he seeks to stir up confusion at every opportunity. Hynes he condemns both for fenianism and (by implication) for being a Castle hack. He damns a "patriot" for selling his country, and he himself has sold out to Tierney, to the clergy, to the English. He keeps on mouthing loyalty to the end, yet always (in the last part of the story) in an appeal to the anti-Parnellian Crofton.

Father Keon represents the degraded political clergy. No ivy hides beneath that disheveled, upturned coat-collar.

Henchy's supreme bit of self-revelation follows Father Keon's exit, when Henchy pictures himself as the wealthy big-shot, lording it over the others. He shows here, in a jest based in bitter seriousness, what his own motivation is, as well as the motivation that ate into the heart of Parnell's Ireland. The self-interest of men like Henchy opposed the life-force symbolized by the ever-green ivy. And the "style" admired by the old man (hardly a thing characteristic of Eumaeus!) covers a dangerous sore on Ireland's body.

Just in passing, I suspect that the boy's asking for the bottles reveals something else about Henchy. He probably deflected the previous consignments to his own profit.

In the presence of Crofton and Lyons, Henchy gives the arguments which appeal to the Conservatives and to the clergy. Crofton (an English sound to that name!) evidently holds the Conservative views, and Lyons presents the clergy's argument against Parnell. Henchy stresses "respectability" and "advantage." In the face of Edward's coming, he puts forth two arguments: 1) it will bring money; 2) fair-play requires that Edward's rakishness be overlooked. How bitter that last argument would taste to a Parnell-man, only those could know who had suffered the agony of Parnell's disgrace, which his enemies did not term "rakishness." And the way that Henchy does it! "He's a jolly fine decent fellow . . . !" Joyce builds the pressure in preparation for the climactic poem.

O'Connor mentions the poem early in the story, and at last asks for it. And Hynes, finally, recites it into the ears of the vile Henchy, the superior Crofton, the respectable Lyons, the weak but loyal O'Connor, the decaying old Jack. It is a masterpiece of a poem. Not by itself, as a work of art, certainly! Affected, puffed up with weak classicism and vulgar bombast, snarled in cliche and mixed metaphors (glorified hounds!), it staggers on through breathless and limping stanzas. But it is *Hynes's* poem, the best product his partially-educated, loving, loyal mind can produce. And his feeling is not swamped by the artistic defects of his poem. Expressing something deeply real in his own heart, he finds an echo in the hearts of the others—"even Mr. Lyons clapped" for *this* celebration of the "immoral" Parnell. Mr. O'Connor can scarcely hide his emotion. But the unspeakable Henchy appeals to Crofton, and Crofton agrees that it is fine, not on the grounds of its emotion, where it is fine, but on the grounds of its writing, where it is pitifully bad. The bitterness and the force of this conclusion are the achievements of a very great artist, who could so well give us the labored pulse of poor Ireland, *sick* with longing for her lost leader, and attacked by filthy little beasts. Perhaps, after all, MM. Levin and Shattuck have a valuable point. At least their thesis may stress for us that Joyce's work will find its counterpart in the greatest and most deeply moving of poetry.

"Clay": An Explication

by Florence L. Walzl

Conflicting elements in Maria, the heroine of James Joyce's "Clay" in *Dubliners*, have led to contradictory interpretations of the character: as saint (William T. Noon, "Joyce's 'Clay': An Interpretation," *College English*, XVII, 1955, 93–95); as thematically disunified combination of laundress, witch, and Virgin Mary figure (Marvin Magalaner and Richard M. Kain, *Joyce: The Man, The Work, The Reputation,* New York, 1956, 84–91); and as unconsciously selfish troublemaker (Richard Carpenter and Daniel Leary, "The Witch Maria," *James Joyce Review,* III, 1959, 3–7). I believe "Clay" is a thematic whole based on a set of contrasts relating to the two church holidays which provide the setting and to the two fortunes the heroine receives in a fortune-telling game.

The setting is Halloween, the night in folk tradition when the dead walk, and (by the anticipation of the heroine) All Saints' Day, a feast honoring all the blessed, both those proclaimed publicly in canonization and those completely unknown to the world. The fact that it celebrates, especially, the unheralded saints of ordinary life has a thematic relationship to the story, as does the walking abroad of spirits on All Hallows' Eve.

The plot of "Clay" is simple. A middle-aged spinster named Maria, a humble kitchen worker in a laundry, spends Halloween with a family, perhaps relatives, for whom she has been nursemaid. While blindfolded in a game of fortunes, she chooses the clay portending death. Her friends quickly hide this choice from her and substitute a prayerbook prophetic of a future convent life. The pathos is deepened by the contrast between the emptiness and futility of her life as it is and as it might have been. For this little laundress has the potential qualities of ideal woman and mother, but their development has been stunted by the circumstances of her life.

In a sense, there are two Marias in this story: the Maria of the laundry and the Maria of the Halloween excursion. Within the confines

"*'Clay': An Explication*" (*original title: "Joyce's 'Clay'"*) *by Florence L. Walzl. From* The Explicator, *XX (February, 1962), Item 46. Copyright © 1962 by* The Explicator. *Reprinted by permission of* The Explicator *and the author.*

of the laundry, several of Maria's qualities, her goodness, peaceableness, and loving motherliness, are greatly stressed. Both as a worker and a person her goodness is evident. She labors to make the scullery of the laundry a pleasant, happy place: the kitchen is "spic and span," the fire "nice and bright," the barmbracks perfectly cut, the plants well-kept. She sees that each laundress is well served at teatime. She spends her hard-earned money buying cakes for the children of the family and plumcake for their elders. Much also is made of her peaceableness. "She was always sent for when the women quarrelled over their tubs and always succeeded in making peace." She always thinks the best of people. The matron of the laundry calls her "a veritable peace-maker." Finally, she is loving and motherly. She evokes the affection of the rough washerwomen who all are "so fond of Maria." She likes to recall the children she formerly nursed who called her their "proper mother." She looks forward happily to the family evening with "all the children singing." Even her name suggests the Church's prototype of the ideal maid and mother in the Virgin Mary. This Maria with her alarm clock set for the early morning mass of All Saints' Day suggests the very kind of saint this feast was inaugurated to honor.

But Maria on her Halloween visitation seems quite different. Though her goodness and generosity within the rounds of the laundry are effective, outside it they are not. In her timidity and lack of experience she loses the plumcake that was to have been her gift to the family and irritates the children over its loss. Moreover, her very presence upsets the adults because they feel the pathos of her life. At one point, Joe's eyes so fill with tears that he cannot find the corkscrew for the family toast. Her peaceableness, which is so marked within the laundry, is also ineffective without. She annoys the salesgirl in the bakeshop, is unable to heal the breach between the two brothers, and unwittingly provokes three near-quarrels: over Alphy, over some nuts, and over her choice of the clay. Also the emotional frustration of her life and its lack of human love are emphasized. Through a series of incidents suggesting romance, Joyce indicates that romantic and maternal love remain undeveloped in Maria. The laundresses' teasing about the ring, the shop girl's suggestion that the plumcake is for a wedding, the gallantry of the gentleman in the tram, and, above all, the verse from "I Dreamt That I Dwelt in Marble Halls" Maria forgets, a verse dealing with marriage proposals—all remind us of the sterility of her life. Finally, her appearance is that of "a very, very small person" with a "very long nose and a very long chin" which nearly meet. This Maria, ineffectual and trouble-making, suggests a Halloween witch.

What is Joyce's intent in this contrast which suggests saint and witch, life and death? I believe the answer is suggested in part by the two

fortunes Maria receives at the party, the prayerbook and the clay—
the first thematically associated with the saints' day, the second with
the Halloween spirits. Both represent her future; both are death
symbols.

The prayerbook, the fortune contrived by the family and forced
upon her, is her immediate future, the life Irish society has molded for
Maria. (In fact, her laundry job had been arranged for her by the
family.) Her life in the laundry is a convent-like existence of narrow
piety and goodness but without spiritual elevation, a life of small
endeavors spent among women of a low class. Yet Maria had the
potentialities for being the kind of heroic woman of full experience
sainthood implies. Celibacy for a person ideally suited for marriage is
a deprivation of life. The prayerbook for Maria is a sterility-death
symbol.

Her hidden fortune, the clay, prophetic of death, suggests all that
the ultimate future holds for her. In combination with Joyce's description of her as a Halloween wraith, it probably suggests also that she is
not fully alive. Prevented by circumstances from full development of
self, she represents virtue in an arrested state. Maria is one of the
living dead of *Dubliners* who like Eliot's Hollow Men are "Shape without form, shade without colour,/Paralyzed force, gesture without
motion."

Structure and Sympathy in "The Dead"

by C. C. Loomis, Jr.

James Joyce's "The Dead" culminates in Gabriel Conroy's timeless moment of almost supreme vision. The fragments of his life's experience, of the epitomizing experiences of one evening in particular, are fused together into a whole: "self-bounded and self-contained upon the immeasurable background of space and time." [1] Initiated by a moment of deep, if localized, sympathy, his vision and his sympathy expand together to include not only himself, Gretta, and his aunts, but all Ireland, and, with the words "all the living and all the dead," all humanity.

Gabriel's epiphany manifests Joyce's fundamental belief that true, objective perception will lead to true, objective sympathy; such perception and such sympathy, however, ultimately defy intellectual analysis. Joyce carefully avoids abstract definition of Gabriel's vision by embodying it within the story's central symbol: the snow, which becomes paradoxically warm in the moment of vision, through which Gabriel at long last feels the deeply unifying bond of common mortality.

Gabriel's experience is intellectual only at that level on which intellect and emotional intuition blend, and the full power of the story can be apprehended by the reader only if he sympathetically shares the experience with Gabriel. As understanding of himself, then of his world, then of humanity floods Gabriel, so understanding of Gabriel, his world, and humanity in terms of the story floods the reader. The understanding in both cases is largely emotional and intuitive; intellectual analysis of the snow symbol, however successful, leaves a large surplus of emotion unexplained.

Therefore, Joyce had to generate increasing reader-sympathy as he

"Structure and Sympathy in 'The Dead'" (original title: "Structure and Sympathy in Joyce's 'The Dead'") by C. C. Loomis, Jr. From PMLA, LXXV (March, 1960), 149–51. Reprinted by permission of the Modern Language Association.

[1] James Joyce, Portrait of the Artist as a Young Man (New York, 1928), p. 249. See also Irene Hendry, "Joyce's Epiphanies" in Critiques and Essays on Modern Fiction, John W. Aldridge, ed. (New York, 1952), p. 129.

approached the vision, but this sympathy could not be generated by complete reader-identification with Gabriel. If the reader identifies himself unreservedly with Gabriel in the first ninety percent of the story, he will lose that critical insight into him which is necessary for full apprehension of his vision. It is, after all, Gabriel's vision, and there is no little irony in this fact. The vision is in sharp contrast with his previous view of the world: in fact, it literally opens a new world to him. If the reader identifies himself uncritically with Gabriel at any point in the story, he is liable to miss those very shortcomings which make the vision meaningful. Yet, in the actual moments of vision, the reader must share Gabriel's view; in a real sense, he must identify himself with Gabriel: "feel with" him.

Joyce, therefore, had to create sympathy without encouraging the reader to a blind, uncritical identification. One aspect of his solution to this problem is a monument to his genius. In the main body of the story, while he is constantly dropping meaningful, often semi-symbolic details which deepen the gulf between the reader and Gabriel, he is also generating what can best be called "aesthetic sympathy"; by the very structure of the story, he increasingly pulls the reader into the story.

"The Dead" can be divided, not arbitrarily, into five sections: the *musicale,* the dinner, the farewells and the drive to the hotel, the scene between Gabriel and Gretta in their room, and, finally, the vision itself. A few of these sections are separated by a time lapse, a few flow smoothly into one another; in all cases, however, the reader is aware of a slight "shifting of gears" between sections.

These sections become shorter as the story progresses. The effect of this constant shortening of scenes, together with a constant speeding up in the narrative line, is an almost constant increase of pace. Within each of the sections, Joyce carefully builds up to a climax, then slackens the pace slightly at the beginning of the next section as he begins to build up to a new climax. The pace in the sections is progressively more rapid, however, partially because of the cumulative effect of the narrative. As the story progresses, more things happen in less time.

The effect of increasing pace is complemented and strengthened by another structural aspect of the story. As the pace increases, the focus narrows. The constantly narrowing focus and the constantly increasing pace complement one another and act to pull the reader into the story. He is caught up in a whirlpool movement, ever-narrowing, ever-faster.

There is much activity in the first part of "The Dead," but the activity is diffuse and the effect is not of great pace. We are given a slightly confused, over-all picture of activity: dancing, drinking, singing, chatter. Characters are introduced one after another: Lily, Gabriel, Gretta, the Misses Morkan, Mary Jane, Mr. Browne, Freddy Malins and his mother, Miss Ivors, and so on. Our scope is broad and general. Increasingly, Gabriel becomes our mode of consciousness, but he himself cannot assimilate all the activity. He retreats, isolates himself within his deep but insecure egotism. Rationalizing that "their grade of culture differed from his," he bides his time until dinner, when he knows he will be the center of all eyes.

In this first section, it is interesting to note how Joyce gives us Gabriel's point of view without compromising his own fundamental objectivity; even though we see largely through Gabriel's "delicate and restless" eyes, we nevertheless become increasingly aware of his character, of his defensive feelings of intellectual and social superiority in particular. His eyes are offended by the glittering, waxed floors, his ears by the "indelicate clattering" of the dancers, his intellect by all those present, particularly Miss Ivors, who "has a crow to pluck" with him, and constitutes a threat to his shaky feelings of superiority. His attitude can best be summed up by his reflection, ironic and revealing in view of the toast to come, that his aunts are "only two ignorant old women." Such comments are introduced quietly, but they serve to keep the reader from identifying himself too wholeheartedly with Gabriel. We feel with him to a degree even in these early sections of the story, but our sympathy is seriously reserved and qualified.[2]

In the second section, our focus narrows to the dinner table, and to a few characters at it; the others are blurred in the background. Tension about Gabriel's toast has been built up in the first section; now the pace increases as this particular tension is relieved. The toast, hypocritical and condescending, makes us further aware of Gabriel's isolation from those around him.

The pace in this scene is considerably more rapid than in the first. It builds up to the climax, the toast, in a few brief pages; then there is a slackening with the applause and singing.

There is a time-lapse between the conclusion of the toast and the next section; Joyce seems to shift to a higher range. From this point to the moment of vision, the pace increases and the focus narrows almost geometrically.

The shouts and laughter of the departure signal the end of the party, but are counter-balanced by the fine, almost silent tableau of Gabriel watching Gretta on the staircase. Our focus is beginning to narrow down to these two main characters. Gretta has been deliberately held in the background until this moment; now she emerges.

The repeated goodnights and the noisy trip through silent, snow-blanketed Dublin are given increased pace through Gabriel's increas-

---

[2] For an enlightening discussion of the problem of reader-identification and "extraordinary perspective" in 19th- and 20th-century literature, see R. W. Langbaum, *The Poetry of Experience* (New York, 1957).

ing lust; the pace becomes the pace of "the blood bounding along his veins" and the "thoughts rioting through his brain." The fires of this lust begin to thaw the almost life-deep frost of his self-consciousness. The superiority and self-delusion are still dominant: there is much irony in his remembering "their moments of ecstasy," for his lust is far from ecstatic love. It is, however, the first step toward the moment of objective vision.

We are now approaching the still center of the increasingly rapid, increasingly narrow whirlpool. The scene in the hotel room between Gabriel and Gretta takes up only a few brief minutes, but in these minutes much happens. Gabriel "discovers" Gretta: suddenly she becomes more than a mere appendage to his ego. He discovers himself, in a mirror. His lust turns to anger, then his anger to humility. Gretta, caught up in her memories of the "boy in the gasworks," Michael Furey, is not even aware of his presence. "A shameful consciousness of his own person assailed him. He saw himself as a ludicrous figure, acting as a pennyboy for his aunts, a nervous, well-meaning sentimentalist, orating to vulgarians and idealising his own clownish lusts, the pitiable fatuous fellow he had caught a glimpse of in the mirror."

The peak of intensity is reached with Gretta's "Oh, the day I heard that, that he was dead." She collapses on the bed, sobbing, and Gabriel, quietly, shyly, retires to the window. At this moment, Joyce creates another time-lapse to lead into the vision itself.

Until this moment, the pace has increased and the focus has narrowed almost constantly. Now Joyce does something remarkable and effective: he reverses the process. In doing so, he makes the structure of the story not only useful as a means of generating an "aesthetic sympathy" (perhaps "empathy" with its impersonal connotations would be a more accurate word), but also makes it reinforce the ultimate emotional-intellectual meaning of the vision itself.[3]

Pace simply ceases to exist in the vision, and, of course, this is fitting. We are in an essentially timeless world at this point; true, the vision involves time and mortality, but it is timeless time and eternal mortality, man's endless fate as man. The snow "falling faintly through the universe" measures absolute, not relative time. The impact of this

---

[3] William T. Noon, S.J., in *Joyce and Aquinas* (New Haven, 1957), pp. 84–85, places Gabriel's epiphany at "the moment when the full impact of Gretta's disclosure of her secret strikes him": before the snow image of the closing paragraphs. Father Noon separates Gabriel's moment of vision from the reader's, and seems to state that the snow image is for the reader's enlightenment, not Gabriel's. I agree with Father Noon that the reader cannot possibly apprehend the depth of Gabriel's sudden sympathy with Gretta until Joyce gives him the closing image, but I do not believe that Gabriel's own vision is complete until this final image; the epiphany begins with his sympathy for Gretta, but is not complete, because not universal, until he "heard the snow falling faintly through the universe."

sudden cessation of pace on the reader is great; in fact, it parallels the impact on Gabriel himself. With this sudden structural change, we share Gabriel's vision; we do not merely analyze it.

Gabriel's vision begins with Gretta; it is narrow in focus. The whole story has led us down to this narrow focus. Now, as he does with pace, Joyce reverses the process. As the vision progresses toward the ultimate image of the snow falling through the universe, the focus broadens, from Gretta, to his aunts, to himself, to Ireland, to "the universe." Time and space are telescoped in the final words of the story: The snow falls on "all the living and all the dead."

"The Dead" follows a logical pattern; we move from the general to the particular, then to a final universal. We see Gabriel's world generally; then we focus down to the particular, and from the combination of the general and particular we are given a universal symbol in the vision itself.

The logic of "The Dead," however, is not the logic of mere intellect; it is the logic which exists on a plane where intellectual perception and emotional intuition, form and content, blend.

Chronology of Important Dates

	Joyce	The Age
1882	Joyce born, February 2.	Phoenix Park murders in Dublin. Trollope, Emerson, and Longfellow die. Wyndham Lewis, Virginia Woolf, and Stravinsky born.
1898–1902	Joyce attends University College, Dublin.	The Boer War; death of Queen Victoria. Irish Literary Theatre founded. Published: W. B. Yeats, *The Wind Among the Reeds*; Freud, *The Interpretation of Dreams*.
1904	Joyce begins *Dubliners*, leaves Ireland with Nora Barnacle.	Published: Joseph Conrad, *Nostromo*; Henry James, *The Golden Bowl*.
1907	*Chamber Music* published (poems written from 1902 onwards).	J. M. Synge's *The Playboy of the Western World* performed.
1914	Serial publication of *A Portrait of the Artist as a Young Man* begins in February; *Dubliners* published in June. Joyce begins *Ulysses*.	World War I begins. Published: D. H. Lawrence, *The Prussian Officer*; Robert Frost, *North of Boston*; Ezra Pound, ed., *Des Imagistes*; Yeats, *Responsibilities*.
1916	*Portrait* published in book form.	Easter rising in Ireland.
1922	*Ulysses* published.	T. S. Eliot's *The Waste Land* published.
1927–29	Joyce publishes early versions of *Finnegans Wake* as *Work in Progress*.	Published: Yeats, *The Tower* and *The Winding Stair*. New York stock market crash ushers in depression.
1939	*Finnegans Wake* published.	World War II begins with German invasion of Poland. Yeats and Freud die.

1941   Joyce dies, January 13.   Germany invades Russia; Japa-
                                             nese attack Pearl Harbor; United
                                             States enters the war. Published:
                                             Woolf, *Between the Acts*; W. H.
                                             Auden, *New Year Letter*; Eliot,
                                             The Dry Salvages.

Notes on the Editor and Contributors

PETER K. GARRETT, the editor of this volume, is Assistant Professor of English at Princeton University. He is the author of a forthcoming study of changing fictional modes from George Eliot to Joyce.

ROBERT BOYLE, S. J., teaches English at Regis College. He is the author of *Metaphor in Hopkins.*

BEN L. COLLINS is Professor of English at Parsons College. He is the author of several articles on Joyce.

DAVID DAICHES is Professor of English and Dean of the School of English Studies at the University of Sussex. He is the author of several literary studies, including *Critical Approaches to Literature* and *A Critical History of English Literature.*

BREWSTER GHISELIN is Professor of English at the University of Utah. He has edited *The Creative Process: A Symposium.*

S. L. GOLDBERG is Professor of English at the University of Sydney, Australia. He is the author of *The Classical Temper: A Study of James Joyce's "Ulysses."*

HUGH KENNER is Professor of English at the University of California (Santa Barbara). He has written several studies of modern literature, including *The Poetry of Ezra Pound* and *The Invisible Poet: T. S. Eliot.*

C. C. LOOMIS, JR. is Assistant Professor of English at Dartmouth College.

FRANK O'CONNOR (Michael O'Donovan, 1903–1966) wrote several volumes of short stories as well as *The Mirror in the Roadway: A Study of the Modern Novel.*

FLORENCE L. WALZL is Professor of English at the University of Wisconsin (Milwaukee). She is the author of several articles on Joyce.

Selected Bibliography

Deming, Robert H. *A Bibliography of James Joyce Studies.* Lawrence: University of Kansas Libraries, 1964.

Background

Ellmann, Richard. *James Joyce.* New York: Oxford University Press, 1959. The definitive biography. See especially Chapter XV, "The Backgrounds of 'The Dead.' "

Gifford, Don. *Notes for Joyce: "Dubliners" and "A Portrait of the Artist as a Young Man."* New York: E. P. Dutton & Co., Inc., 1967. Annotates facts and allusions in each story.

Criticism

Gibbons, T. H. *"Dubliners* and the Critics," *Critical Quarterly,* IX (Summer, 1967), 179–87. Questions the validity of recent symbolic interpretations.

Hart, Clive, ed. *James Joyce's "Dubliners": Critical Essays.* To be published early in 1969. New studies of each of the stories.

Levin, Richard, and Charles Shattuck. "First Flight to Ithaca: A New Reading of Joyce's *Dubliners,"* in *James Joyce: Two Decades of Criticism,* ed. Seon Givens, pp. 47–94. New York: Vanguard Press, Inc., 1948. Argues that *Dubliners* is based on parallels with the *Odyssey.*

Magalaner, Marvin. *Time of Apprenticeship: The Fiction of Young James Joyce.* New York: Abelard-Schuman Limited, 1959. Discusses the evolution of *Dubliners,* examines early versions of the stories.

TWENTIETH CENTURY
INTERPRETATIONS
Maynard Mack, *Series Editor*
Yale University

NOW AVAILABLE
Collections of Critical Essays
ON

A Portrait of the Artist as a Young Man
Samson Agonistes
The Scarlet Letter
The Sound and the Fury
Tom Jones
Twelfth Night
Utopia
Walden
The Waste Land
Wuthering Heights